TRAINS 1921–1939

STRATUS

ADAM

JOŃCA

POLISH ARMOURED TRAINS 1921–1939

VOL. 1

Published in Poland by
STRATUS s.j., ul. Żeromskiego 6A
27-600 Sandomierz, Poland
e-mail: office@mmpbooks.biz
as MMPBooks
e-mail:rogerw@mmpbooks.biz

http://www.mmpbooks.biz

ISBN
978-83-67227-35-3

Editor in Chief: Roger Wallsgrove
Editorial Team: Bartłomiej Belcarz, Artur Juszczak, Robert Pęczkowski
Author: Adam Jońca
Cover: Dariusz Wyżga
Layout Design: Bartłomiej Belcarz
Translation: Artur Przęczek
Proof-reading: Konrad Przeczek

Printed by
Wydawnictwo Diecezjalne
i Drukarnia w Sanodmierzu
www.wds.pl

PRINTED IN POLAND

Photographs: the author's collection, Tomasz Basarabowicz, Bogusław Bobel, [the late] Pascal Danjou, Jacek Haber, Artur Przęczek, Sławomir Kordaczuk, Dariusz Kowalczyk, Krzysztof Kuryłowicz, [the late] Janusz Magnuski, Paul Malmassari, Krzysztof Margasiński, Wawrzyniec Markowski, Mariusz Zimny, *Centralne Archiwum Wojskowe* (*Wojskowe Biuro Historyczne*) – Central Military Archives (Military Historical Bureau), *Archiwum Dokumentacji Mechanicznej* (*Narodowe Archiwum Cyfrowe*) – Archives of Mechanical Documentation (National Digital Archives), *Ośrodek "Karta"* – The "Karta" Centre, *Muzeum Wojska Polskiego* – Polish Army Museum, *Muzeum Historyczne w Legionowie* – Historical Museum in Legionowo, *Muzeum Niepołomickie* – Museum of Niepołomice.

Colour profiles: by the author – based on technical reconstruction drawings by Artur Przęczek, [the late] Witold Jeleń, [the late] Leszek Komuda and the author.

Special thanks to Mr. Artur Przęczek for creating and providing reconstructions of technical drawings of rolling stock, coaches, wagons and steam locomotives.

Translator's notes: the abbreviation P.P. – *pociąg pancerny* (armoured train) is applied throughout the book. The names of the individual armoured trains are retained in Polish. The abbreviation *wz.00 – wzór*" (issue / model) distinctively identifies any given piece of military equipment by the year of introduction.

INTRODUCTION

Armoured trains were extremely crucial weapon systems in the Polish-Ukrainian War of 1918–1919 and the Polish-Bolshevik War of 1919–1920. The dominating feature of both wars was manoeuvrability – hardly ever the battle-lines were truly defined. In mobile warfare with unstable fronts, combat trains were a formidable and effective weapon.

The exact number of armoured trains created in the period 1918–1921 cannot be established. There were several dozen of them – some operated for a very short time. The names, numbers and assignments changed, as well as the rolling stock composition. Some trains were assembled from whatever materials and armaments were at hand, and were described as armoured trains in a somewhat optimistic manner. Sometimes they did not even appear on the official weapon registries.

Depending on what criteria is applied, in total there were 85, maybe even 90 Polish combat trains. Those days and those trains require a special study – it is being prepared and will be released in the not too distant future. It will be the volume **"Polish Armoured Trains 1918–1921"**, in the same format and with the same narrative method as in this publication.

This volume begins in 1921 – after the war with Soviet Russia – and ends in September 1939 – the German invasion, followed 17 days later by the treacherous Soviet attack, thus starting a new Great War, this time designated as number "Two".

In a separate study, we plan to present armoured trains, undoubtedly Polish, but not belonging to the Polish Army. Such are the Polish trains of the I Corps formed in Russia in 1917, so when the Independent Republic of Poland had not yet existed, and the trains from Arkhangelsk and Novorossiysk, allied to the Entente, and formally belonging to the Polish Army in France, a separate Polish armed force combined with the Polish Army in the country only in September 1919.

"Polish-non-Polish" were also trains of the Central Lithuania army existing as a separate state from October 1920, after the so-called rebellion of *Generał* Lucjan Żeligowski, joined to the Polish in April 1922. The Army of Central Lithuania was an autonomous formation, under its own command.

The situation of Polish trains in the Wielkopolska Uprising was similar, although for different reasons. The Autonomous Greater Poland Army began to merge with the Polish Army in December 1919. Before that time, and after the victory of the uprising, the Greater Poland Army was operationally subordinate to the orders of the Polish Army, but inside it governed itself.

In Silesia, during the Third Uprising, the insurgent army was subordinate to the Supreme Command of the Insurgent Forces and only after the victory the Silesian armored trains formally became trains of the Polish Army, and the temporary I. Upper Silesian Armoured Train Regiment was disbanded only in 1923.

In September 1939, 10 regular armoured trains went into battle; a few improvised trains were created during the September Campaign.

To those who unwisely claim that armoured trains were wasted money and misused equipment assets, since even a single enemy aircraft could easily disable this obsolete weapon system... it is worth remembering, that these mobile four-gun artillery batteries – that is what in fact the armoured trains were – managed to inflict considerable losses to the enemy. It is also worth to emphasize that the P.P. 54 "*Groźny*" – the train with the shortest combat history – was not eliminated by the enemy, but only by a bridge that was prematurely blown up by retreating Polish troops. Armoured trains P.P. 53 "*Śmiały*", P.P. 55 "*Bartosz Głowacki*" and P.P. 51 "*Marszałek*" were in full working order after three weeks of defensive fighting. Armoured train P.P. 52 "*Piłsudczyk*" also remained in operation for three weeks and was intentionally derailed by the crew when the ammunition supply was exhausted. In the course of the campaign, in a single encounter, P.P. 53 "*Śmiały*" was able to demolish a large number of the German *Panzer Division* tanks during the battle of Mokra.

While it is true that anti-aircraft defences of the Polish armoured trains were inadequate, an addition of the modern "*Bofors*" 40 mm anti-aircraft gun allowed for a success in fending off enemy aerial assaults. Both, P.P. 51 "*Marszałek*" and P.P. 55 "*Bartosz Głowacki*" were supplemented by such guns during the campaign.

During the course of the 1939 defensive war, there was an enormous effort on part of the armoured train crews to dissolve huge railroad traffic jams. Many track repairs were very efficiently carried out – the training paid off.

So let us do justice to the heroic actions of the crews and pay tribute to the armoured trains of the Polish Army...

TABLE OF CONTENTS

TECHNIQUE AND ORGANISATION

P.P. 2 "Generał Sosnkowski" *during the exercises of the* 1. Dywizjon Pociągów Pancernych *(1st Armoured Trains Group) in 1933.*

History in Brief

Arguably, the first use of railroad equipment for military purposes took place in 1846 in the vicinity of Vienna, when a "shielded" – cannon armed – flat railcar, pushed by an ordinary steam locomotive, was used for reconnaissance purposes. Some two decades later, during the fighting of 1866 in Italy, and then during the Franco-Prussian war, "protected trains" were deployed again. Meanwhile, in United States of America, in the course of the Civil War, armoured trains were also used, and – it is worth noting – they were of an advanced technical standard compared to their European counterparts.

Railroad artillery is also an American invention from the era of the Civil War – the Confederates first used heavy 32-pounder cannon on a four-axle flat railcar.

Towards the end of the XIX century – in the 1880's France, Britain and Russia begun to design and develop special artillery wagons – sometimes protected by armour – equipped with the medium and large calibre cannons. One such railroad battery was used in combat in 1889 during the Romanian defence of Siret (Seret).

In 1899 and 1900, during the Boer War, the British used trains with armoured infantry wagons and armoured locomotives to defend Mafeking and Ladysmith – the Boers, not well armed and without artillery, could not quite cope with them.

In the Russo-Japanese War, Russia made use of cannon-armed trains protected with sandbags and wooden railway sleepers (ties).

During the Great War of 1914 there was a vast deployment of railway rolling stock which undoubtedly could be classified as armoured trains – protected with steel plates, armed with cannons and machine guns. German trains supported the advance through Belgium. In the East, the Russians deployed their trains into battle, while the fighting in the Carpathians was supported by Austro-Hungarian trains.

At the Western front, where the battle lines soon froze to a stalemate in the trenches, the technical development of the armoured trains came to the halt.

The extraordinary increase in the amount of artillery and resulting firepower in conjunction with advanced abilities to reconnoitre allowed for precise shelling of any given enemy position. Therefore, with heavy artillery dominating the area, an armoured train might not have been able to even approach the front lines and

Above and opposite page: *"Smok" armoured train. It was a regular train of the Polish Army designated as Number 7 – in a technical sense it was an improvised train. It was employed as its design permitted – as a "half-armoured" patrol train. It was formed in December 1918 in Nowy Sącz as the "Smok"* Krakowskiej Baterii Kolejowej L.4 *("Smok" of the Cracow Railway Battery L.4). It operated on the Przemyśl – Lwów railway line, later it was transferred to Cieszyn in Silesia. At the end of 1919, it was disbanded due to poor armour and armament. Most armoured trains resembled this kind of layout in the fighting of 1918–1920 – goods wagons were armoured with concrete poured in wooden frameworks, machine gun and small arms ports were placed in the side walls of wagons, an armoured steam locomotive was sometimes only partially protected. The upper photograph, taken in the spring of 1919, depicts "Smok" with the wagons of the supply section coupled to the combat train – it was a common sight in the Polish-Ukrainian War. It was not possible to leave an unarmed administrative section in a safe place, because there were, in fact, no secure zones. The threat was not only Ukrainian regular units, but also ordinary bandits.*

engage the enemy with its explicitly lighter guns. Quite likely, it would have been damaged or destroyed during the advance.

After the war, Germany – the Weimar Republic and the *Freikorps* troops – formed combat trains (largely improvised), used against the communist revolt in Westphalia, in liquidating the Bavarian Soviet Republic around the vicinity of Munich in 1919, and in rebelling Upper Silesia.

The circumstances for trains in Russia were somewhat different. Vast and empty spaces, almost completely devoid of good roads resulted in the extensive use of railways.

The period of the Soviet Civil War and the concurrent war with Poland, contributed in a special way to the development of the equipment and tactics of armoured trains. Armoured trains were used by both "Whites" and "Reds" factions as well as by Ukrainian, Estonian, Latvian, Lithuanian troops and all other nations breaking the subordination to defunct Russian and Austria-Hungarian empires.

The first Polish armoured train was probably a set of two steam locomotives and eight wagons protected with railway sleepers (ties), put together in February of 1863 during the January Uprising, and to be more precise, deployed during the fighting against the Russians over the railway station in Sosnowiec. In truth, the train was not actually involved in combat – it only served as means of protected transport for an insurgent unit from Maczki to Sosnowiec.

Before Poland regained independence, the *I. Korpus Polski* (1st Polish Corps) formed in Russia, around February of 1918 at Bobrujsk, assembled an improvised train called "*Związek Broni*" – armed with a 76,2 mm gun and machine guns, with "armour" consisting of sandbags. In mid-March, the train was augmented by a captured flat railcar carrying an immobile "*Austin*" armoured car.

Short time later, a second improvised train was set up. A third train was added after the 1st Corps captured a railway anti-aircraft and anti-balloon battery during the attack on Osipowicze on 19 February. Eventually, in accordance with the conditions of the capitulation, on 10 May 1918 all three trains were taken over by the German Army.

In August 1918, the Polish artillery training battery from Murmansk found itself in Arkhangelsk alongside the British intervention forces. The gunners created two improvised trains – No. 1 and No. 2, which operated on the Arkhangelsk-Vologda railway line. In late October 1918, both trains were handed over to the White Army.

In July of 1918, Polish *5. Dywizja Syberyjska* (5th Siberian Division), begun the

Above and right: Two photographs of the front wagon of "Smok" with an ordinary field gun limited to fire along the track, only slight sideways aiming of the gun was possible.

Below: Two images of the "Smok" locomotive, of Austrian origin, Series 229.49 (also known as the Nowy Sącz VIII type).

construction of three trains – "*Kraków*", "*Poznań*" and "*Warszawa*". In winter, when the division was withdrawing to Vladivostok, they covered the evacuation. En route, at the Taiga railway station, the "White" train of the Kolchak Army was captured and was given the name "*Poznań II*". In January 1920, after the division's capitulation, the trains were handed over to the Red Army.

The beginnings of the resurrected state of Poland were marked by the acute lack of resources. Retreating Russians transported back into Russia everything that could have been pillaged away. The withdrawal of the German troops was no different. Poland inherited ruined infrastructure and robbed factories, and almost immediately, the inevitable armed struggle to define the borders.

The first Polish train was an Austro-Hungarian armoured train that was seized on 1 November 1918 in Prokocim, a suburb of Cracow. The train was deployed to protect the relief transports sent to Przemyśl. Only after the town had been re-taken from the Ukrainian forces, the equipment was divided into two separate trains ("*Śmiały*" and "*Piłsudczyk*"). In the following few days both units set off to fight for Lwów (nowadays Lviv in Ukraine). This Austrian armoured train was not an improvisation; it was a technically advanced weapon, thoughtfully designed and built for combat.

Constructors of the new Polish trains – desperately needed for the front – tried to apply Austrian (and Russian) solutions to some extent, but by necessity, they could only build what was possible,

The second locomotive assigned to "Smok" *– Austrian Series 73 Number 415.*

and to make matters worse, in a hurry. Armour plates were unavailable, so the protection had to be achieved by means of concrete (sometimes just sand) poured into wooden frameworks, reinforced by railway sleepers (ties) and rails. Former German and Austrian trench shields were also used when available. The steam locomotives and wagons used to assemble the trains were often in poor condition. The armament consisted of various, sometimes archaic, weapons – many hardly suitable for combat.

The third Polish armoured train, built in Lwów, *Pociąg Pancerny* 3 – P.P.3, also known as the "*Pepetrójka*" (original name "*Lwowianin*", later renamed to P.P.3 "*Lis-Kula*"), was, in fact, improvised at first. It had, among other cannons, a Russian mountain gun shooting Austrian ammunition. The situation was so desperate that the artillery shells had to be machined beforehand so that the calibre of the gun and rounds was more or less the same. The wagons of "*Pepetrójka*" were relatively quickly refined at the Lwów railway workshops, and in a short time com-

An Austrian-built covered wagon converted for combat. In the firing port a barrel of a gun may be noted – most likely an old fortress 9 cm cannon, possibly taken from the casemates of the Przemyśl Fortress.

The composition of the standard-gauge armoured train P.P. 10 "Pionier", built around January and February 1919 at workshops in Lwów – photograph from May 1919. Machine gun wagons are typical goods wagons with 10 cm thick concrete covering and gun slits. Both of artillery wagons, front and rear, are the first Polish-built artillery wagons with rotating turrets, (armed with 8 cm casemate cannons Model 1894 *from the forts of Cracow) which enabled them to fire to the sides (sector of fire approximately 240°). The artillery wagons were converted from steel German coal wagons of the Ommku series. An Austrian steam locomotive* Series 178 *with both the boiler and engine driver's cabin armoured. In September 1919, the train was reinforced with a 122 mm Russian howitzer. The rolling stock of the administrative supply section consisted of about 30 wagons.*

Photographs showing one of the two artillery wagons of "Pionier" *with a cannon in a rotating turret.*

KRECHOWIAK

A fine example of war booty armoured train. It is a train designed and built as an armoured unit, not an improvised modification from civilian rolling stock. Its history very well illustrates the complicated events of the eastern borderlands of the Republic of Poland. The Russian armoured train "Chunchuz No. 1" *was knocked out by Austrian artillery at Rudoczka near Równe (today Rivne in Ukraine) in September 1915. The wreckage remained in "no man's land" for a long time, until the Russians managed to pull it from the battlefield and repair it in the summer of 1916. During the turmoil of the war, in the autumn of 1918, the train, at the time as a* "Tovarishch Voroshilov" *belonging to the Bolsheviks, was captured and incorporated in the forces of the Ukrainian People's Republic as the* "Sichovy" *train. On 24 May 1919 it surrendered in Radziwiłłów to the 2nd Squadron of the* 1. Pułk Ułanów *(1st Lancers). Once it was re-launched, it was initially named* "Krechowiak". *As a regular train, it was given the Number 20 and a new name* "Generał Dowbor-Muśnicki" *(broad-gauge). In the late spring of 1920, the train covered the retreat from Ukraine – it was destroyed in combat on 6 June, between Fastowo and Koziatyn. It was wrecked when rammed and thrown down from the embankment by an unmanned locomotive sent forward at full speed by the Bolsheviks.*

Opposite and above:
The captured Ukrainian "Sichovy" *armoured train commemorative photographs taken while still named* "Krechowiak", *with the troopers of the 2nd Squadron of the* 1. Pułk Ułanów Krechowieckich.

Top right and right:
Photographs taken after the official incorporation into the Polish Army as P.P. 20 "Generał Dowbor-Muśnicki".

GENERAL

Seen from the side – the armoured locomotive and artillery wagon of "Generał Dowbor-Muśnicki".

The left side of the artillery wagon of "Generał Dowbor-Muśnicki".

Opposite page:
Russian armoured locomotive of the O[W] *series of* "Generał Dowbor-Muśnicki".

pletely replaced with new, better designed and better protected ones.

The period from the end of 1918 throughout almost the entirety of 1919, was the time of building improvised trains, adjusting and developing technical abilities, as well as refining the tactics. The advantageous circumstances at the time were such that on both fronts, the Ukrainian and Bolshevik, the Polish Army was dealing with poorly organised opponents – individual enemy formations, sometimes large in numbers, but not able, or not willing to cooperate with each other.

The period dating from the end of 1919 – the time of the onset of the Polish-Soviet War, introduced new challenges. The Bolsheviks deployed an army that was fairly well organised and better armed, and also commanded by a cadre of "Red" officers, who were by that time seasoned in combat. But the Polish experience gained, in both technical and tactical aspects, as well as the rebuilding of railway workshops and enhancing construction abilities began to pay off. Polish trains were getting better and more advanced. Although in some respects, they were still inferior to most of the Russian ones – built in well-equipped factories and made of proper, not substitute materials. The Polish Army acquired several Russian trains in the course of the war – and they were valuable assets. In March 1919, the Polish Army had 18 regular armoured trains, plus at least a few provisional ones, but the number continuously grew. Trains were captured from the Ukrainian Galician Army (standard-gauge), Ukrainian People's Republic (broad-gauge) and the Red Army (broad-gauge). In mid-August

"Generał Dowbor-Muśnicki" *decorated with Christmas tree garlands – New Year 1920 (also a good illustration of the huge problems with the coal supply).*

1919, Polish Army had 22 regular armoured and 18 provisional trains. However, there were also losses – two trains were lost in 1919.

At the beginning of 1920, as modern equipment was continually delivered some older wagons and provisional trains were phased out, so Polish Army had 14 regular standard-gauge and 9 regular broad-gauge armoured trains, a total of 23 battle-worthy units.

In the summer of 1920, Polish armoured trains covered the army's retreat – suffering heavy losses. These losses were hastily replaced, so that in September there were 27 regular trains in service. After the final cessation of hostilities (in October 1920), 28 trains are listed in the documents dating from the end of November.

It is difficult to determine how many trains were concurrently in service during those two years, because apart from regular armoured trains, there were also improvised trains, sometimes deployed for only a few days. There were also major changes in the rolling stock – wagons and locomotives which were worn out, damaged or obsolete were replaced. Interestingly, the name of the train was appended to the crew rather than the rolling stock. So the naming convention of some trains included the annotation "1st forming", "2nd forming", and sometimes even the "3rd forming", when the crew lost their train or new equipment was introduced.

Combat Composition

In the period of 1918–1920, the method of assembling combat wagons was developed. It was primarily dictated by the availability of rolling stock, but also by military practice.

The locomotive was usually placed in the centre of the train. At the front, there was a flat railcar (without brakes),

The control flat railcar loaded with sleepers and rails for possible track repairs – P.P.16 "Mściciel" *armoured train, Rudnia Oholicka, September 1919 (in the front artillery wagon a Russian 3-inch field gun may be noticed).*

followed an artillery wagon with a cannon of 75 to 100 mm calibre, wagons with machine guns and light guns able to fire sideways, infantry wagons, and behind the locomotive additional infantry wagons. At the end of the train there was a second artillery wagon. The artillery wagons of improvised trains usually had an ordinary field gun facing forward. Due to the length of such a weapon, greater than the width of wagon, the traverse of fire was limited to more or less 60°. Therefore, quite quickly, following the designs of the well devised Austro-Hungarian and Russian trains, the construction of wagons with guns in rotating turrets was developed.

In the 1920's this general arrangement was streamlined, but kept in place, so until the war of 1939 the combat composition was arranged in the following order: front flat railcar, front artillery wagon, locomotive, an assault wagon with machine guns, rear artillery wagon, and the rear flat railcar.

Flat Railcars

The typical composition of the armoured train included a leading flat railcar, the so-called control railcar, also known as the combat platform. Initially, depending on availability, different types of flat railcars were used for this function. The front flat railcar to some extent protected the succeeding combat wagons from derailment due to the tracks damage, for example a land mine explosion. It could also serve as an equivalent of a naval fireship (brander), decoupled while in motion and sent ahead of the train, possibly packed with explosives, it could inflict damage to an enemy train on the track ahead.

In the 1920's, the American made four-axle flat railcars were most commonly used. In the second half of the 1930's, the 13.1 m long *Pdkz* flat railcars built in Poland were found to be most appropriate and adopted as a standard.

The *Pdkz* series railcar ("*P*" – for flat railcar, "*d*" – for load capacity of 15–20 tons, "*kz*" – for iron stanchions), also referred to as *Pdks* ("*s*" – for carrying rails), had two axles. The length of the loading area made it possible to carry the rails and turnout components necessary for repairs of damaged tracks. The standard Polish light-type rails, best suited for immediate repairs, had a length of 12 m as dictated by the climate.

The flat railcars, both from the army's own resources and those delivered on mobilization by *P.K.P.* (*Polskie Koleje Państwowe* – Polish State Railways), were of Polish production, according to the *C-VIII* pattern, which was the equivalent of the German type *C143*. In the *1. Dywizjon Pociągów Pancernych* (1st Armoured Train Group), flat railcars intended to be used as frontal ones were modified by adding stowage boxes for screws, spikes, anchors, fishplates, etc. The compartments with hinged doors were installed in open spaces within the frame, under the flat railcar floor.

During the ordinary (travel) march an observer was positioned at the front. The flat railcar itself had no brakes, but a cable was connected to nearest valve in the following wagon so that the observer could activate the braking system without delay in case of danger or, for example, in the event of running too close to the train's draisine.The rear control flat railcar, just like the front one, was of the *Pdks* type, but since in the *1. Dywizjon* there were only six flat railcars converted with stowage boxes, and in the *2. Dywizjon* there were none (it had its "own" five *Pdks* and two *Pddk* flat railcars) – the commercial flat railcars of this series, were provided by *P.K.P.* during mobilization.

An Austrian field gun on a front flat railcar (with wooden stanchions). The wagon closer to us – a low-sided coal wagon – has an Austrian 8 cm Model 1894 *cannon, with the capability of firing sideways. A photograph was taken from the locomotive tender. The train is the* Krakowska Bateria Kolejowa L.3 "Gromobój" *(Cracow Railway Battery L.3* "Gromobój"*) formed in December 1918, which later would become P.P. 6* "Gromobój".

Front Artillery Wagon

The front artillery wagon was coupled behind the control flat railcar with a double coupling. In a single turret wagon, the gun barrel was facing forward, and in a two turret wagon, the lower gun turret pointed forward. The main armament of the wagon was complemented by machine guns in the side wall slits and, later, an anti-aircraft machine gun in the turret on the top of the wagon. In the *1. Dywizjon*, only the "*Śmierć*" armoured train had two-axle, single turret artillery wagons – the remaining trains had four-axle wagons with two gun turrets each. In the *2. Dywizjon* it was "*Bartosz Głowacki*" that had single turret artillery wagons.

Rear Artillery Wagon

It was the second wagon armed with a gun and / or howitzer. All the wagons were four-axle, equipped with two rotating turrets – except for two trains listed above. In the 1930's, after final reorganization and unification of combat wagons the front and rear artillery wagons were identical, except for the "*Paderewski*" and "*Groźny*" armoured trains.

Armoured Train Artillery

With time, the initial armament mosaic was systematically sorted out, which was necessary, because different gun systems and calibres resulting in the requirements for varying ammunition caused enormous logistical problems. At first, artillery wagons built in Nowy Sącz, Cracow or Lwów had Austro-Hungarian guns, often obsolete, largely taken from the forts of Cracow and Przemyśl. The combat wagons coming form Poznań and Warsaw had German and occasionally Russian artillery pieces.

After the Polish-Soviet War, Russian 3-inch guns – designated as *wz. 02* ("*wzór*" – issue / model) of 76.2 mm calibre and Russian 122 mm (48-line, model 1909) howitzers were adopted as the standard equipment for armoured trains.

In the late 1920's, another universal replacement of armament was initiated.

Above: A 75 mm wz. 02/26 *gun in the* "Sormovo" *type turret. Such turrets were installed on the captured armoured trains manufactured at Sormovo – originally they mounted Russian 76.2 mm Model 02 and Model 14 guns.*

Left: An Austrian casemate cannon positioned to provide the sideways field of fire (standard-gauge P.P. 12 "Kaniów" *armoured train, formed in January 1919, lost in the war with the Bolsheviks on 14 July 1920).*

Instead of the Russian 3-inch guns, the 76,2 mm *wz. 02* guns, a modified improved version was installed – *wz. 02/26*. These were guns adapted to the French designed ammunition of 75 mm calibre – the same as used in the Polish field artillery cannons *Schneider wz. 1897*. The Russian 122 mm howitzers *wz. 09* were also abandoned in favour of the 100 mm *Škoda* howitzers *wz. 14/19*.

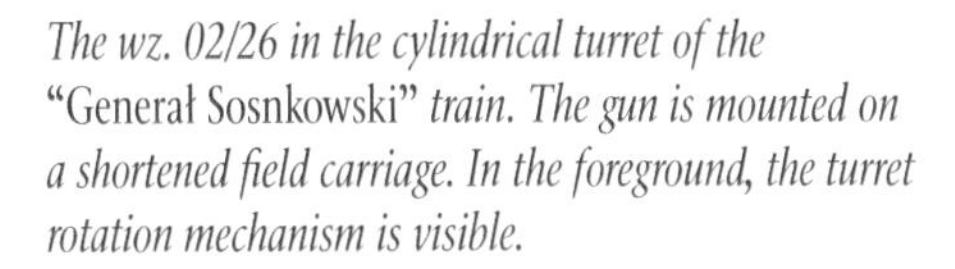
The wz. 02/26 in the cylindrical turret of the "Generał Sosnkowski" *train. The gun is mounted on a shortened field carriage. In the foreground, the turret rotation mechanism is visible.*

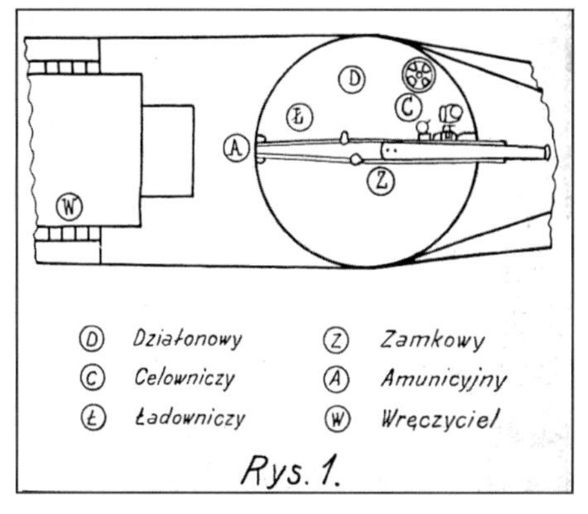

The wz. 02/26 in the cylindrical turret of the "Generał Sosnkowski" *train. The gun is mounted on a shortened field carriage. In the foreground, the turret rotation mechanism is visible.*

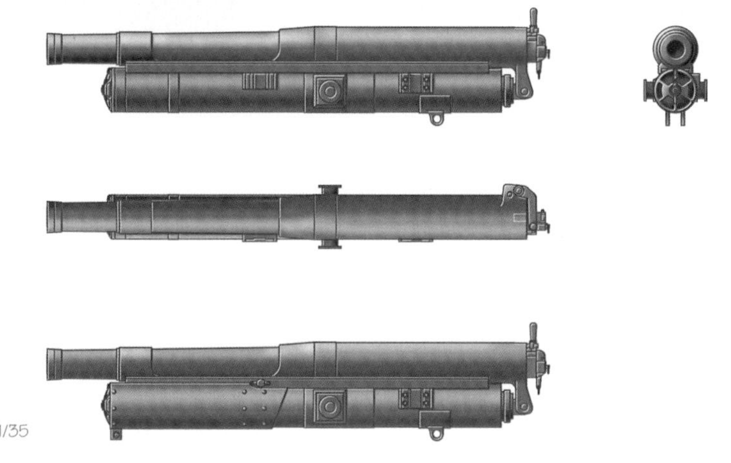

The 75 mm gun wz. 02/26. Bottom drawing depicts a variant with armour protection on the recuperator cowling.

Left: The "Sormovo" *turret with the wz. 02 gun (wagon Number 460025 from the* "Groźny" *train).*

The 100 mm howitzer wz. 1914/19A. The upper drawing – without armoured covers, both drawings below with covers for the hydraulic recoil cylinder (recuperator) in two versions.

A wz. 02/26 gun mounted on the naval type mounting in the "Sormovo" *turret – the mount could still be used after the earlier wz. 14 gun barrel had been removed.*

A wz. 02/26 gun mounted on the naval type mounting in the "Sormovo" *turret; the side view.*

Automatic Weapons

After the initial period, during which every weapon that could be obtained was valuable, for instance – Austrian, German, Russian, American, British and French (from the wartime supplies to the Russian Army), it was also time to standardise this type of armament. The Maxim *wz. 08* machine guns of German design were selected for use in armoured trains – robust, but heavy and complicated to maintain – they were still quite appropriate, because their large weight was irrelevant, and the chance of dust or mud jamming their mechanism were much smaller than in the field.

In the late 1920's, rotating turrets for the Maxim *wz. 08* were mounted on artillery wagons as anti-aircraft weapons. Some wagons already had heavy machine gun turrets – they were dismantled and replaced with new ones, of a standard type.

An Austrian machine gun wz. 07/12 on a field mount, placed on a specially made wooden bench – P.P.5 "Odsiecz" *of the 1st forming. Formed in November 1918 as* Krakowska Bateria Kolejowa L.1 *(Cracow Railway Battery L.1), from covered goods wagons and low-side coal car. Disbanded in October 1919 – the main reason was very poor armour protection and insufficient armament.*

A typical drum mount removed from the wagon's firing slit with a heavy machine gun wz. 08.

Below: A drum mount installed in a flat vertical steel wagon side.

A drum mount installed in a flat vertical side of a wagon planked with wood.

A drum mount in profiled "barrel" type walls, installed vertically (initially, on the trains which had such arched side walls, the mounts were inclined in the same way as the curvature of the wall – this made shooting difficult, and was later modified to an upright position). In the second photograph, the heavy machine gun is taken out of the mounting drum and stowed in a rack for travel.

The interior of a rotating anti-aircraft turret with a heavy machine gun wz. 08. Such turrets were installed at the end of the 1920's on all artillery wagons.

Cropped and enlarged section of a photo of the "Poznańczyk" *train (around 1928). The assault wagon with early* "T" *shaped type antenna masts.*

Assault Wagon

The assault wagon also referred to as a sortie wagon, sometimes an infantry wagon – was intended to transport a sortie platoon and pioneers. The wagon had four heavy machine guns in the side walls embrasures. The soldiers of the combat platoon were armed with *wz. 98* carbines, hand grenades and a Maxim *wz. 08/15* light machine gun (a second gun of the same model was stored in the command post on the locomotive tender). Shortly before the outbreak of World War Two, the Maxim *wz. 08/15* was replaced with a Polish *Browning wz. 28* machine gun build under licence.

There was also wireless communication equipment in the wagon. The first to receive a radio was the "*Danuta*" armoured train. Two masts with horizontal spears (T-shaped) with antenna wires stretched between them were placed on the roof of the assault wagon of this train. It could not be determined what type this first radio set was.

In the period of 1932–1939, the standard wireless equipment of the armoured trains were radios with the military designation *RKD/P* (factory designation *AW*), designed and manufactured at the *Państwowe Zakłady Tele – i Radiotechniczne* (National Tele and Radio-communication Research Facility) in Warsaw. This equipment was designed to work with continuous wave telegraph (A1 emission) and telephony (A3 emission) in the medium wave range. During a halt, it provided two-way communication over a distance of 50 – 80 km, and in motion a range of some 10 to 15 km. The transmitter contained three vacuum (electron) tubes, and was powered by a *CWS 02P* combustion electric generator in conjunction with an 8 V accumulator. The receiver had five electron tubes and was powered by a 120 V anode battery and a 4 V accumulator. The main part of the aerial antenna was the 25 m long copper tube, supported by wooden masts installed on the roof.

The wireless set, in accordance with the term: *RKD – Radiostacja Korespondencyjna Dywizji* (Divisional Correspondence Radio-station), was intended for communication with the headquarters of the units to which the armoured train was assigned.

The RKD wireless set. It was enclosed in a wooden box. A generator and an accumulators were separate elements.

Training of communications platoon in the 2. Dywizjon Pociągów Pancernych *(2nd Armoured Train Group) – handling field telephones and switchboards.*

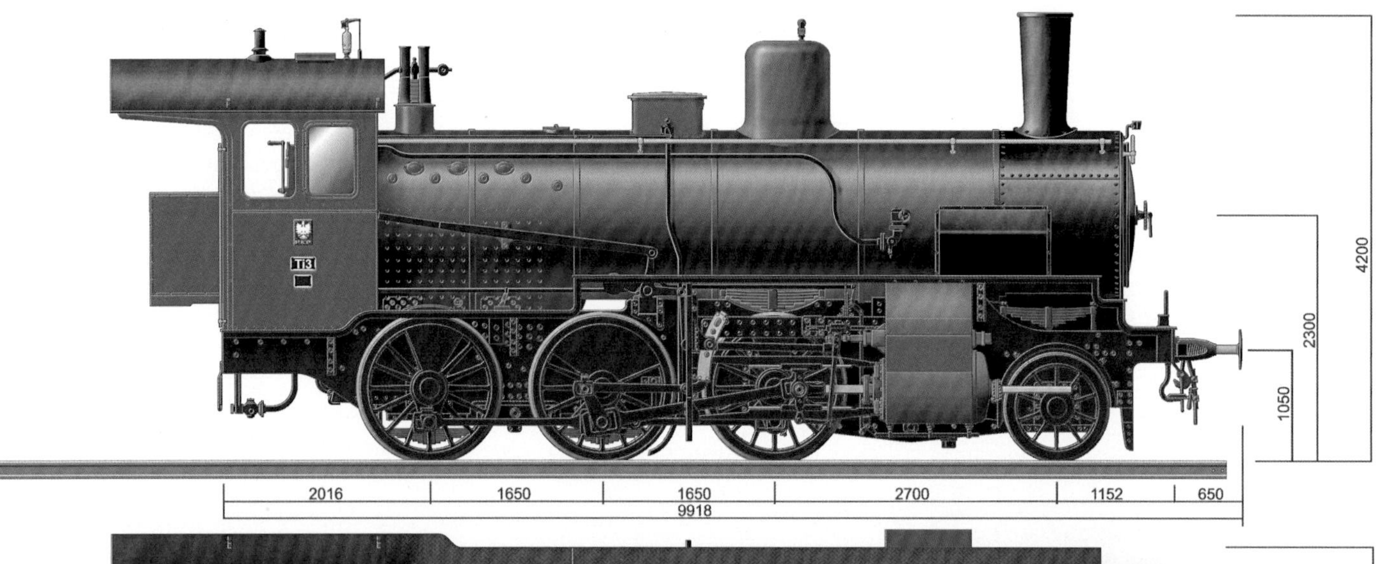

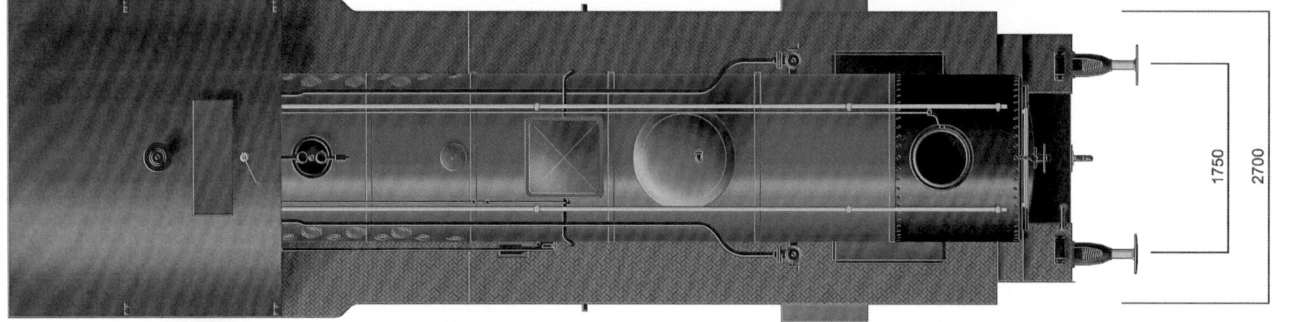

Armoured Steam Locomotives

In the period of 1918–1920, over 50 steam locomotives had been armoured at the following workshops: Lwów – 16, Stanisławów (presently Ivano-Frankivsk in Ukraine) – 2, Nowy Sącz – 12, Kraków – 8, Wilno (nowadays Vilnius in Lithuania) – 2, Poznań – 3, Warsaw – 8, Zdołbunów – 1 Russian broad-gauge steam engine.

In addition there were captured steam locomotives of the Austrian Series *377* and the Russian broad-gauge O^{W} series.

There was quite an array of types: Austrian Series *73* steam locomotives were armoured (7 for certain, possibly more), Series *178* (6 locomotives), Series *229* (at least 11), Series *180.5* (1 steam locomotive), Series *97* (probably no more than 2) and Series 5^4 (most likely just 1); in addition there were Prussian Series *G3* (several), $G5^1$ and $G5^2$ (a few), $G5^3$ (at

A goods and passenger locomotive of the Prussian $G5^3$ series – Polish designation Ti3.

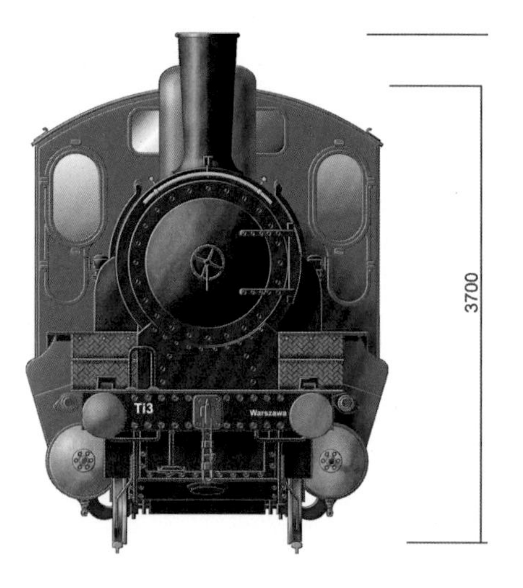

least 2), *G5*[4] (probably 1 or more), *G7*[1], *G7*[2] and *G8*[1] (several), as well as German tank locomotives *T9*, *T11* and *T16*.

In 1926, a decision was made to standardise the type of steam locomotives for all armoured trains. The choice fell on the ex-German locomotives of the *G5*[3] series, which received the Polish designation *Ti3* ("*T*" – for cargo, "*i*" – for axle arrangement oOOO, "*3*" – for 3rd series of Prussian origin). These steam locomotives were almost identical – "almost", since even though of the same design (*Musterblatt*), they came from various manufacturers and from different years of production, therefore minor alterations were implemented. The *G5*[3] series were locomotives of the so-called *G5* Group (*Guterzuglokomotive Gruppe 5*). The group consisted of five variants referred to as series, marked from 1 to 5. They were used by the Prussian state railways and in small numbers by the Mecklenburg and Alsace-Lorraine railways. A significant number of *G5* locomotives were built, almost 1500. The coal tenders attached to the locomotives, under Polish nomenclature designated as *12C1* ("*12*" – for 12 m³ capacity, "*C*" – for three-axle, "*1*" – for Prussian origin), were also armoured. In the 1st Armoured Train Group there was also one *16D1* four-axle tender (16 m³ capacity, four axles, Prussian origin). The armoured train command post was arranged in the armoured superstructure above the tender.

The standardisation of steam locomotives in the railway troops (*Ti3* locomotives also became a standard equipment assigned to the railway engineers) obviously facilitated the functioning of the combat and support units. The crew training was simplified, as the steam locomotives had identical steering mechanisms, parameters and manoeuvrability features, so was the maintenance of the engines. In all, the most important factor was that the costs were kept down. It is worth to mention that for the periodically reoccurring (required for safety reasons) internal inspection of the boiler, which included a water pressure test, some of the armour had to be removed. The presence of various types of locomotives and different armour arrangements and patterns would significantly increase the costs. To further improve the feasibility of the operations, a directive was issued to coordinate the inspections with the required semi annual wear component replacements, both minor and major.

The *Ti3* steam locomotives began entering service in 1926, successively replacing previously used engines. The withdrawn equipment was returned to the *P.K.P.* Most locomotives were deployed in the regular civil service; some unsuitable ones were scrapped, while what was considered as the quality armour was stored as a mobilization reserve depots.

Electro-combustion Wagon *wz. 28*

In 1928, an armoured, self-propelled vehicle was built according to the design of the *Biuro Konstrukcyjne Broni Pancernych* (Armoured Weapons Design Bureau). It was armed with a 75 mm gun and heavy machine guns. In principle, it was a standard gauge artillery wagon with a combustion electric drive. In the perspective envisioned by the designers it was to form a train when coupled with a second armoured wagon and two flat railcars. Such a set would be an equivalent of an actual light armoured train.

The idea of building self-propelled artillery wagons kept coming back from time to time. One of the last interesting concepts dating back to 1936 was developed at the *Zakłady Ostrowieckie* (Ostrowiec Works). It was combustion engine – electric motor armoured artillery wagon with a single gun turret and a typical heavy anti-aircraft machine gun turret. Two heavy machine guns mounted in the sides and four heavy machine guns in the front and rear for firing along the track supplemented the main armament. The proportions of the gun turret suggested that an armament of up to a 100 mm howitzer could be installed. The wagon was conceived as an element of a combat train that could consist of three motorized 20 ton armoured wagons and two towed 15 ton flat railcars.

Rear view of the electro-combustion wagon wz. 28 with open entrance door (exercises in Pilawa in 1934).

Diesel-electric Locomotive

The project of a diesel-electric locomotive (armoured electro-locomotive) for pulling armoured trains with a total weight of up to 110 tons was developed in 1931. The requirement specified that the locomotive would be able to tow a train consisting of two armoured wagons and two 15-ton flat railcars with a total weight of over 100 tons. The propulsion system was to consist of two *Saurer BLD* diesel engines coupled with *Brown-Boveri* generators and electric motors powering the wheel axles.

The three axle locomotive prototype was finally built in 1932 at the Lilpop, Rau & Loewenstein facility in Warsaw. Soon after, the trials began and lasted at least until the end of 1933.

In 1934 the locomotive was redesigned to have a four-axle arrangement. At the beginning of 1938, a chassis with a drive, vacuum brakes and a provisional mock-up wooden body was built at the Cegielski Plant. The locomotive remained under testing until the outbreak of World War Two.

Above left:
Side view of the electro-combustion wagon wz. 28.

The wz. 28 *electro-combustion wagon during the exercises in Pilawa in 1934.*

The locomotive's control panel.

Above: A prototype of the diesel-electric locomotive at the Zegrze railway station.

A prototype of the diesel-electric locomotive coupled to a wagon of the "Poznańczyk".

Armoured Draisines

The idea for an armoured train to be preceded on the move by a small, armoured reconnaissance vehicle resulted from the experiences of the war in the eastern Polish borderlands in 1919–1920. A scout vehicle moving in front of the train could reconnoitre the condition of the track and warn of any threats – damage or mines, it could also check the condition of bridges and culverts and provide alert of any suspected ambush attempts.

At the beginning of 1920, ten small French *Crochat* cargo draisines were brought to Poland with the intention of arming and armouring them. Nothing came of this, because the engines were too weak – the idea was abandoned and the draisines were placed at the disposal of railway engineers.

The same year, the attempts were made to buy cars adapted to running on rails, which could have been a good solution if they were capable of being fitted with armour or if they were actual armoured cars. To some extent such a solution was already proven, as former Russian rail armoured cars were still in use during the Polish-Ukrainian fighting in 1919. This initiative also did not work out, and, as the war was over the matter of the draisines ceased to be urgent.

The idea was revisited at the end of 1924. Twelve battle worthy and most technically advanced armoured trains remained in service so it was decided to purchase and armour twelve draisines. A national competition for the design of an armoured draisine did not produce worthwhile solutions which led to the decision purchase them from abroad.

Model building is timeless – soldiers of the workshop platoon of the 2. Dywizjon *show off their model of an* Austro-Daimler *draisine.*

In 1926, the possibility emerged to acquire draisines designed at the Czech *Ringhoffer-Tatra* factory.

Meanwhile, in 1927, two *Austro-Daimler* motor passenger draisines were purchased. For a short time they served in the *Dywizjon Szkolny* (Training Group). Most likely only one of them got armour protection. They clearly did not live up to expectations, because there was no "sequel" and we do not even know what happened to them in the 1930's.

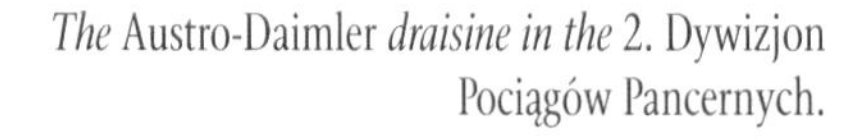

The Austro-Daimler *draisine in the* 2. Dywizjon Pociągów Pancernych.

Armoured Draisine *Tatra*

Six complete draisines were purchased in Czechoslovakia and delivered to the military in November 1926. Even before the delivery took place, in September 1926 an additional contract was signed for the acquisition of nine chassis, which were intended to be armoured in Poland.

The six draisines were evenly distributed between both Armoured Train Groups stationed in Jabłonna and Niepołomice.

According to new rolling stock roster dating from 1930, the *1. Dywizjon Pociągów Pancernych* from Jabłonna had the following trains: P.P. 1 "*Danuta*", P.P. 2 "*Generał Sosnkowski*", P.P. 3 "*Paderewski*" and P.P. 4 "*Śmierć*" – equipped with *Tatra* draisines. As the *1. Dywizjon*, initially had only three draisines, a fourth draisine had to be transferred from the *2. Dywizjon Pociągów Pancernych*. Thus, in the *2. Dywizjon*, only two draisines were left and they were assigned to the P.P. 5 "*Śmiały*" and P.P. 6 "*Groźny*".

Arming of *Tatra* draisines in Poland was eventually abandoned. The chassis were stored and considered a maintenance reserve. In the late 1930's, worn out chassis of the three *Tatras* were replaced with those in storage. Only one armoured body was built – its components were eventually used for the major overhaul of one of the active *Tatra* draisines.

"Tatra" *draisine Number 103 shortly after having arrived in Poland.*

A Tatra *draisine in the 1. Dywizjon – with the* Hotchkiss *heavy machine gun set up for firing at ground targets, in the photograph below with a heavy machine gun in the top hatch for anti-aircraft fire.*

363 Br. Panc.

Tatra *draisine Number 102, painted overall grey with white name* "Żuk". 1. Dywizjon Pociągów Pancernych, *1927.*

A Tatra *draisine of the* 2. Dywizjon.

A Tatra *draisine in the* 2. Dywizjon.

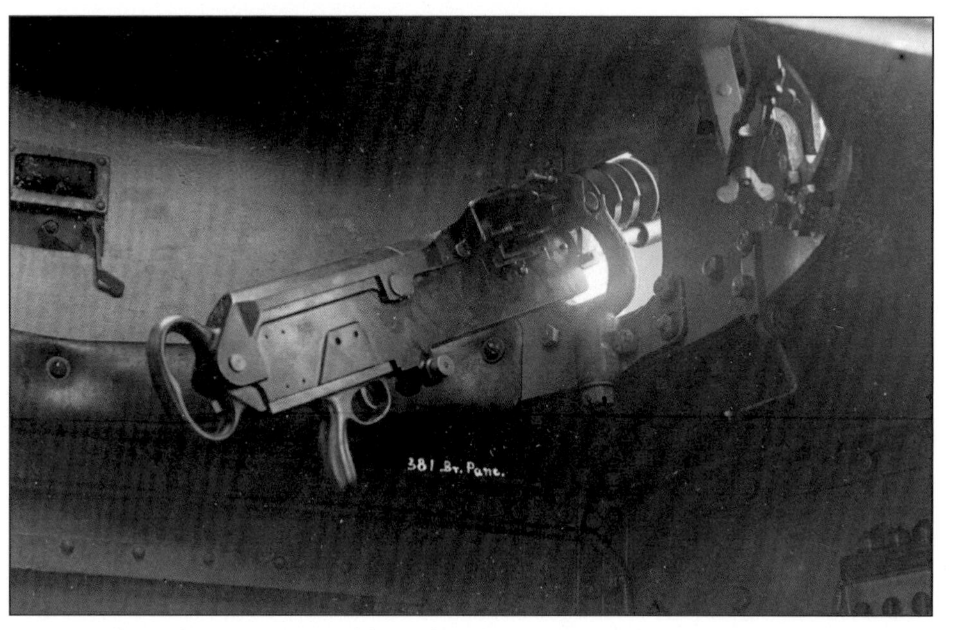

Above and next page: Images of the Hotchkiss *heavy machine gun mounted for firing at ground targets.*

Two photographs of the Hotchkiss *heavy machine gun mounted in the top hatch of a turret.*

Armoured Draisine *R*

The *Tatra* draisines were limited to the rails and could scout only along the track, so the matter of reconnaissance in the field and establishing a forward artillery fire control post remained unsolved.

A good solution turned out to be the so-called "armoured track and terrain draisine". Other nomenclature used: "*średnia drezyna pancerna torowo-terenowa R*"– "medium armoured track-terrain draisine R", "armoured draisine track-terrain R", or "R rail auto-transport". It was a frame equipped with railway wheels designed to carry a *Renault FT* tank armed with a 37 mm gun (*char canon*).

The intent was to provide a railway chassis (carrier frame) that would be powered by the tank's engine for rail travel, but which would allow the tank to drive off and go in the field.

The first chassis, designed at the *Wojskowe Biuro Badań Inzynierii* (Military Bureau of Engineering Research) in 1931, was built in 1932 at the workshops of the *1. Dywizjon Pociągów Pancernych* in Jabłonna. It was actually a "functioning mock-up", made using craftsman rather than manufacturing techniques, with all connections made by means of bolts and nuts, without riveting and welded joints – which allowed for easy replacements of modified components during development. Primarily, the objective was to determine if it was possible to effectively transfer the power of the tank directly from its tracks, without altering the tank itself.

Upon entering the rail guide, the tank rested on fairly large rollers with resembled solid rubber tires. The axles of individual rollers were connected with a system of gears, and the axle of the front roller transmitted the rotation to the axle of the front rail wheel set.

An "iron" (soft-metal) tank from the *Centralne Warsztaty Samochodowe* (Central Automotive Workshops), build for training purposes, was used for the tests. The tracks were modified to use short link plates. The new tracks with more plates than the orig-

First prototype of the R *draisine.*

This image depicts the first prototype of the R draisine, photographed at Jabłonna in 1932.

Both photographs above: The first prototype of the R draisine, front and rear view.

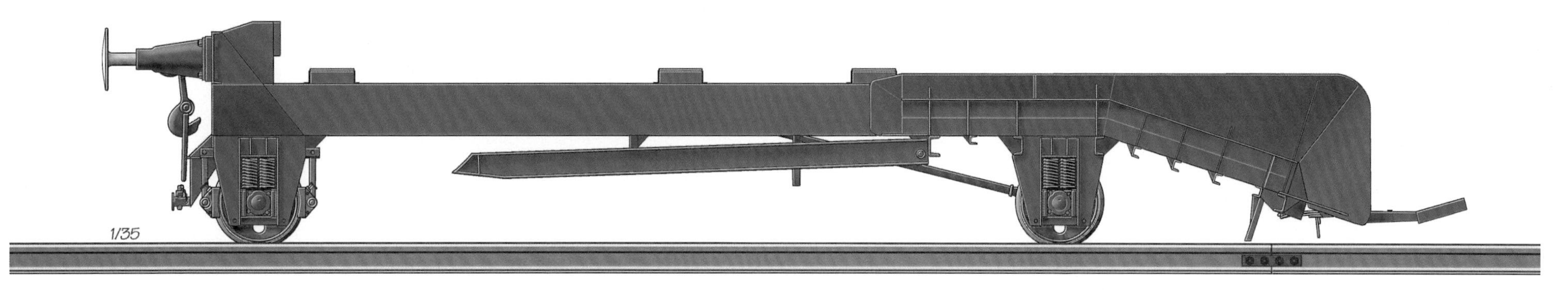

The standard R type rail guide.

The R draisine – one of the very early versions of the prototype, with small bogie wheels and without grease-boxes on the axles of the wheels.

Above: A photograph of an early production rail guide, without armoured covers on the grease-boxes.

An early production R draisine. The bamboo antenna mast seems to suggest that the tank is equipped with a wireless set, but it is doubtful.

inal long link ones provided better contact with the rollers. The drive worked well – the tank on the rail guide frame reached a speed of 38 km/h, but the overall reliability of the system was low, since the wear of bearings, rubber and tank drive elements was definitely excessive.

The subsequent proposal for a technical solution of the draisine's propulsion was different. The engine of the tank was also used to power the system, but the driving force was transferred to the rear wheel set of the carrier frame by means of a special attachment connected to the tank's engine. It constituted of an extension of tank's gearbox and a cardan (universal joint) shaft connected to gear box on the split axis of the rail guide's rear wheel set. The time needed to disconnect the cardan shaft and get the tank off the frame was about three minutes, the time needed to enter the rail guide and connect the shaft – about five minutes. The unit with a *Renault FT* tank had a traction force of 25 tons, which allowed for the coupling of the *TK-R-TK* set, in which the *R* draisine was a tug for two connected tankette rail guides carrying *TK-3* or *TKS* tankettes.

In combat, the tanks could drive off the rail guides onto the ground for reconnaissance or train protection. Typically, the *FT* tank remained on the rail guide, maintaining visual and telephone communication with the tankettes or with the forward observer's post, and if necessary supporting the tankettes with the fire of its gun. The cramped interior of the *Renault FT* tank made it impossible to fit the wireless communication set inside. However, some *R* draisines with an antenna mast are visible in the photos. At least two *R* draisines were equipped with radio compartments located between the stringers of the entrance ramp.

A TK-R-TK *set. The* TK-3 *tankettes are equipped with bamboo antennae masts.*

The R *draisine with a wireless set compartment located between the ramps of the rail guide.*

Light Armoured Draisine *TK*

It was also decided to develop a railway guide for the *TK* and *TKS* tankettes. However, the issue of the propulsion was solved in a completely different way than in the *R* type draisine.

The rail guide for the tankettes was a very simple structure. It was a frame – made of two U-shaped truss beams fastened with crossbars. Small wheel bogies with leaf springs were attached to the crossbars. Two hinged guide ramps (centred over the rails and supported in horizontal position by a spring) were placed in the front. An inside girder and its hydraulic lifting mechanism were also suspended on the crossbar.

The tankette, after driving backwards onto the rail guide, was above the rectangular girder which could be raised to make contact with the bottom of the tankette in order to lift it. For driving, the girder was locked in lower position, so the tracks touched the rails. The tankette rode on its own tracks, and the rail guide, as its name implied, restrained the tank, preventing it from sliding off the rails. When two such rail guides were coupled together, the girder of one of them was raised to the upper position so the tracks of the lifted tankette did not touch the rails. The power of one tankette was enough for movement

– the second was pulled or pushed while suspended. This arrangement of coupled guides was called a *TK-TK* set.

In everyday practice, two *TK-R-TK* sets were assigned to one armoured train. A system in which two *TK* guides were coupled with an *R* draisine carrying a *Renault FT* tank, one at the front and second one in the rear. During a secured march, one *TK-R-TK* set was moving in front of the train, reconnoitring the area, while the other set covered the train from the back or was coupled to the train if the rear was considered to be secure. If the direction of movement was reversed, the rear unit automatically assumed the role the leading one.

The prototype of the *TK* draisine was built in 1932 – a few more were built by 1936. After further developmental changes and improvements, the rail guides were introduced to the armoured trains as the "*lekka drezyna pancerna torowo-terenowa TK*" ("*TK* light armoured track and all-terrain draisine"). In October 1936, a batch of 38 rail guides was ordered from the Lilpop, Rau & Loewenstein factory.

In July 1939, the *Kierownictwo Zaopatrzenia Broni Pancernych* (Armoured Armament Supply Directorate) intended to order 12 more *TK* guides – which, of course, had never materialized due to the outbreak of the war.

Opposite page, above: A TK-3 *tankette with a rail guide during a presentation of Polish military equipment in Romania in 1935.*

Opposite page: An early production TK *rail guide with a* TKS *tankette.*

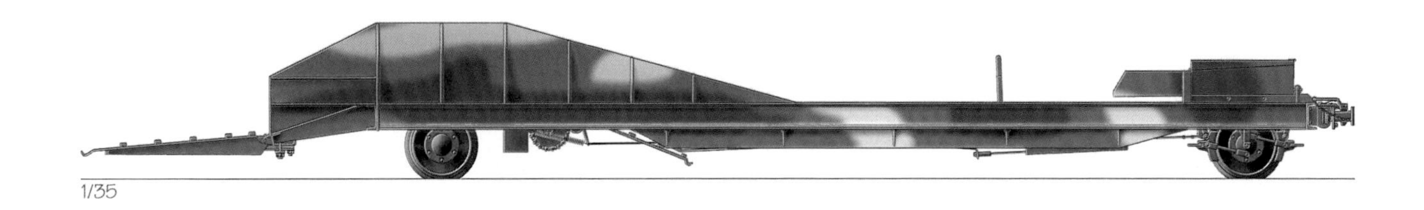

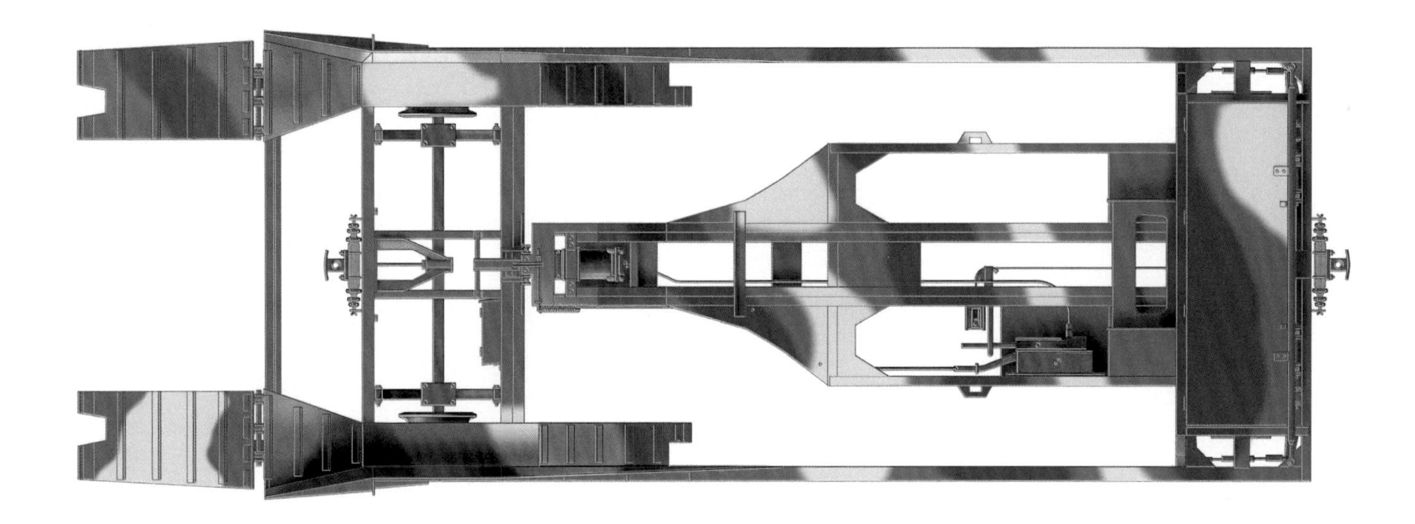

Drawings of the early production TK *rail guides. The drawing below depicts a later version, with strengthened stringers and arched wings of the ramps.*

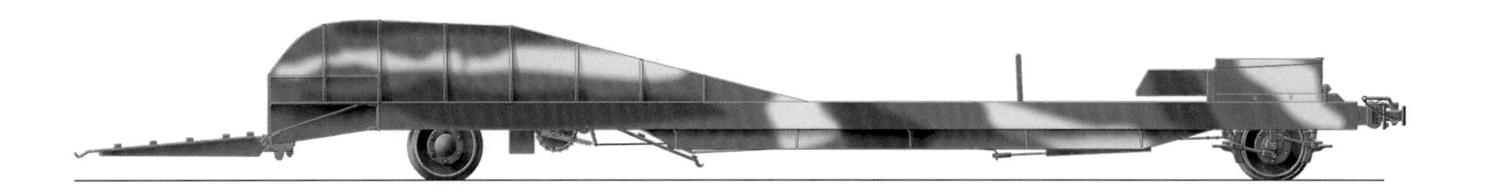

Tankette with a Wireless Radio-set

In the platoon of draisines, in each *TK-R-TK* set, one of the tankettes was to be equipped with the *RKB/c* wireless communication set that would enable radio-telephonic communications between the tankettes and the armoured train. However, it was not implemented in all of the draisine platoons.

The wireless set consisted of a *RKB/c wz. 34* tank short wave transmitter, a *RKB/c wz. 34* receiver, power sources (a DC converter, two converter accumulators, a glow accumulator, an anode battery), the necessary cables and enclosures, and a bamboo antenna mast. Audio communication between two *RKB/c* wireless sets, under average operating conditions, was possible up to a distance of 5 km when stationary, and 1.5 km on the move. Without charging the power sources, the transmitter could work continuously for 4 hours, the receiver – at least 150 hours.

The installation of the wireless set involved conversion of the tankette's interior – but not very extensive. Before the radio-stations in the tankettes were designed, in 1935 attempts were made to try another solution – motorcycles with wireless radio-transmitters and a *Citroën-Kegresse* half-track fitted with wireless set were tested as field reconnaissance equipment. Radio-stations on the motorcycles had proved successful. Not so much the half-track, not because of the radio, but because of the faults and poor technical condition of the vehicle.

A TK-3 *tankette after leaving the railway guide.*

A TK-3 *tankette equipped with a wireless set.*

A TK-3 tankette with a wireless set, photographed in Legionowo (a balloon hangar can be seen in the background).

TKS radio equipped tankettes, left and right side view.

A TK-3 tankette with a wireless set, antennae mast down and up.

A radio equipped TK-3 tankette seen in a photograph taken during the military equipment show in Romania.

Light Armoured Draisine TK with a TKS tankette with a wireless set, Legionowo.

Tankette *TKW*

The big disadvantage of the *TK* draisines was the fact that the tankette on the rail guide could only fire forward, along the track, with a 20° field of fire to the left and right in case of the *TK-3*, and 25° in case of the *TKS* tankette. In order to shoot outside of these sectors, the tankette had to drive off the rail guide.

At the end of 1932, a rotating turret with a heavy machine gun was installed on a specially adopted hull of a *TK* tankette. Due to the configuration of the interior, the turret had to be offset to the right side of the vehicle. The tests of the prototype had demonstrated that the shift of the tankette's centre of gravity had a negative impact on its behaviour during the move. The machine gun mount was found to be defective, but more importantly the visibility was terrible, crew communication difficult and the ventilation very poor. Subsequently, the turret was redesigned to include an improved weapon mount, a reversible periscope and an air vent at the top... But the serious deficiencies remained unchanged – impaired crew communication and an overload of the right side of the vehicle. As a result, at the beginning of 1935, the idea of tankette fitted with a turret was finally abandoned.

The first prototype of a tankette with a rotating turret (with a Browning heavy machine gun)

In both photographs below, the modified TKW *tankette prototype can be seen – with an air vent on the top of the turret and a new mount for the heavy machine gun.*

Armoured Draisine 7TP

For all practical purposes the concept of the *R* draisine was very satisfactory, but a new rail guide was needed for the *7TP* tank – better armoured, with a more powerful engine and an excellent anti-tank gun, but at the same time three tons heavier. There was also a need for a *C7P* tractor (derivative of the *7TP* tank) rail guide, which would be useful for railway engineer companies.

The design largely echoed the technical solutions of the *R* draisine. The prototype carrying a *7TP* tank (or interchangeably a *CP7*) could travel with a maximum speed of 60 km/h, and could tow up to 60 tons of rail vehicles.

The Cegielski factory technical staff participated in the construction of the prototype, and later observed the trials, as the plant was to build the railway guides upon an order from the army. The delivery and the first trials of the prototype took place in July 1936. A summer exercise with the so-called "*autotransport czołga 7TP*" – "auto-transport of the 7TP tank" was performed in the *1. Dywizjon Pociągów Pancernych* with very good results. In September 1936, the rail guide was tried again in the *1. Dywizjon*, but this time the tank was armed and manned by a qualified crew from the *3. Batalion Pancerny* (3rd Armoured Battalion). After the tests, the rail guide remained in storage at Legionowo.

A new model of the rail transporter (carrier) designed for 7TP tanks or C7P tractors.

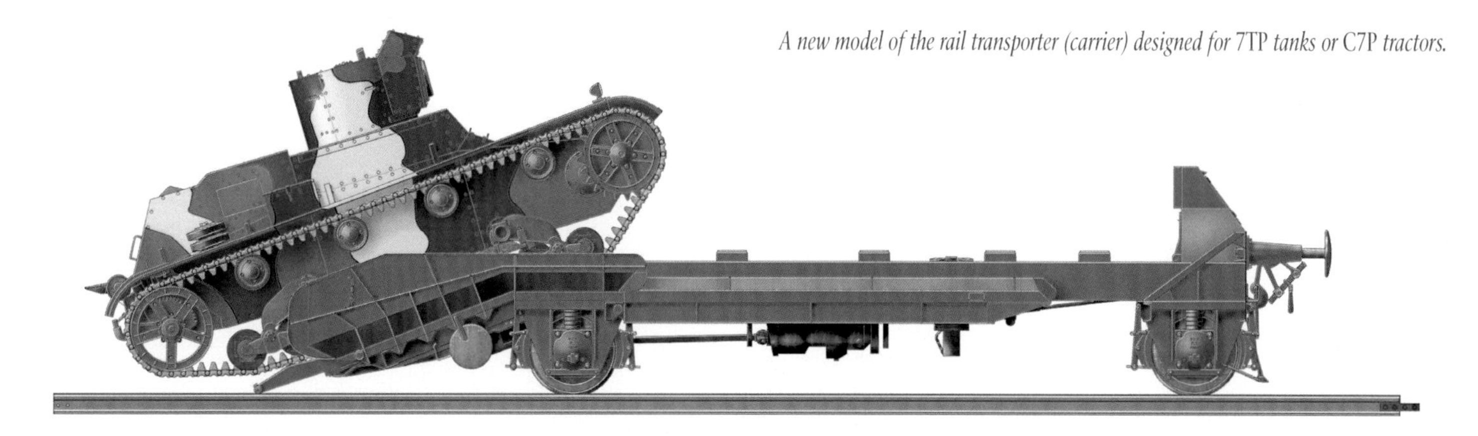

7TP tank on the ramps of a railway carrier chassis.

All photographs: The new type of rail carrier chassis photographed during trials in Legionowo, 1936.

287 Br. Panc.

Motor Vehicles

Slowly but inevitably, the motorization was introduced to the military railroad units. In 1924, in the newly formed *Dywizjon Ćwiczebny Pociągów Pancernych* (Armoured Trains Training Group) riding horses were provided for the upper echelon officers. Referred to as "governmental" or "government treasury", the horses were intended for the group commander, his second-in-command and adjutant, train commanders (there were three active trains, the remainder was considered as a mobilization reserve), train artillery platoon commanders and their deputies.

The initial introduction of mechanical equipment included a motorcycle with a sidecar at the disposal of the group commander. Three bicycles for messengers of the train commanders' sections were added. The transport service in the armoured train group was still performed by three carts and six draught horses.

The situation changed over time. The armoured trains groups received the *FIAT 15ter* and *SPA* light trucks to replace the horse-drawn carts. The ageing *Harley-Davidsons* were replaced with Polish production *CWS* motorcycles and, in time, additional *Sokół* 1000 motorcycles with sidecars as well as a smaller *Sokół* 600.

The number of motorized vehicles was still far too modest to fulfil the real needs. It was also necessary to replace some of the vehicles in use – the *SPA* light trucks and some of the archaic *FIAT 15ter*

Standard issue CWS *motorcycle serviced in the* 2. Dywizjon Pociągów Pancernych.

Ursus-SPA *lorry, 1,5 t.*

Polski Fiat 508 "Łazik".

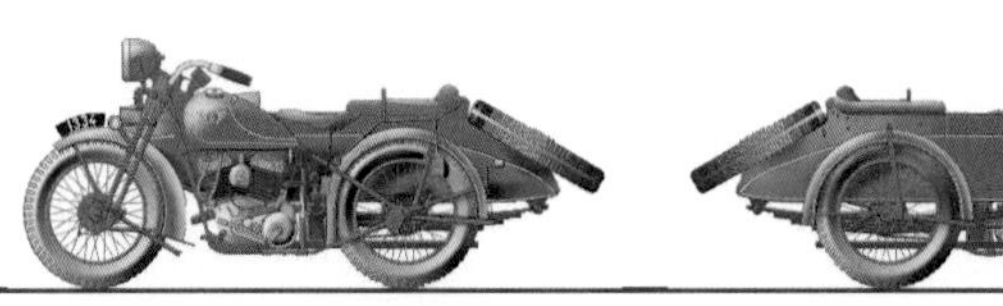

Sokół 1000 *motorcycle with a sidecar seen from the left and right sides.*

A half-tracked lorry wz. 34, *1.6 t.*

Half-tracked lorries wz. 34 *on rail guides.*

trucks were already completely worn out by the 1930's. Attempts were made to achieve such an arrangement that each train would have one or two lorries and two motorcycles in the supply echelon section, and two additional motorcycles in the combat section (carried on the rear flat railcar). This goal was almost fulfilled during the mobilization of 1939. Some trains were even assigned an all-terrain *Polski Fiat 508 "Łazik"* cars.

An antiquated and heavily dilapidated FIAT 15ter *light truck from the motor pool of the* 1. Dywizjon Pociągów Pancernych, *in 1934.*

Vehicles Adapted for Rail Travel and Rail Guides

All-terrain vehicles on rail guides could be particularly useful in the eastern borderlands – where the road network was preposterously inadequate, and the railway lines were the most important communication routes. Even the maintenance roads often running parallel to the tracks could be a serious challenge for ordinary cars.

Rail guides for the *wz.34* half-tracked lorries were to be introduced as a permanent part of an armoured train composition. After disengagement from the rail guide, these vehicles could operate freely on the ground. For track movement, the front of the vehicle was raised and attached to a cradle like trolley with railway wheels. A second trolley, equipped with a lift, was attached to the rear of the *wz.34* half-track frame. The drive was provided by the tracks resting on the rails. Another version of the rail guide system was designed in such a way that two vehicles were coupled back to back. Depending on direction of travel the unit moved using the engine of one or other of the vehicles. The fronts of the trucks were placed on single-axle trolleys with railway wheels. At the rear, between the vehicles there was a 4-wheel rail trolley with retractable pillars supporting the end cross beams of the vehicle chassis. The tracks of the leading vehicle sat on the rails, those of the towed vehicle were suspended above the rails by means of a chain.

The first version was abandoned almost immediately, while the second rendition did not arouse much enthusiasm either. A meeting of the commanders of both armoured trains groups in 1937 concluded that while all vehicles serving armoured trains should be modified to drive on the railroad tracks and on the ground, the rail guides of the *wz. 34* half-tracks had too many disadvantages and "did not perform reliability in operation".

There were also quite successful attempts to place other motor vehicles on rails. In the *2. Batalion Mostów Kolejowych* (2nd Railway Bridge Battalion), two old *Pierce-Arrow* lorries were adapted at the workshop to move on rails, there were also tests of an *SPA* lorry in which the pneumatic tyre wheels were replaced by pressed sheet metal wheels with a flange. Up until the outbreak of World War Two, which interrupted all work, *Polski Fiat 508* "*Łazik*" was tested with

Opposite and above: To the equal extent, both the railway engineers and the commanders of armoured trains were interested in motor vehicles adapted to move on tracks. Railway engineers from Legionowo converted two Pierce-Arrow *lorries into rail tractors at their own workshops.*

A Pierce-Arrow *cargo truck supported by a jack positioned in the centre of gravity – this method allowed to rotate the vehicle in order to change its direction of travel.*

positive results, and an adaptation of the *Sokół 1000* motorcycle was also carried out. It can be easily assumed that these vehicles would have joined the armoured trains as there was a great deal of interest from the officers.

An SPA lorry during tests of driving on tracks. On the left, the vehicle on lifts, on the right, in the process of installation of the railroad wheels with flanges.

Representatives of armoured forces during the tests of an SPA lorry on the railway type wheels with flanges.

First attempts to adapt the wz. 34 half-tracked vehicles for railway use.

ARMOURED TRAINS 1921 – 1923

Following page: 4 September 1920 in Nowy Sącz – a newly commissioned armoured train named P.P.25 "Stefan Czarniecki". *The composition was changed later that month when a wagon with a searchlight was transferred to the* "Huragan" *train. The two-turret artillery wagon remained with the train until its decommissioning, and, in 1933, the gun turrets and parts of the armour were used to construct a new artillery wagon for the armoured train* "Paderewski". *The single-turret artillery wagon was converted into an assault wagon, and in 1930 it became part of* "Generał Sosnkowski". *The last wagon to the left, visible in the photograph, had its machine gun turret replaced by one of a surplus observation turrets taken from the tender of one of the locomotives; the armour arrangement of the sides remained practically unchanged – the wagon stayed in the reserve of the* 2. Dywizjon *and in 1939 was included in the Exercise Train of the Reserve Detachment of the 2nd Armoured Train Group* (Ośrodek Zapasowy Pociągów Pancernych).

Opposite page: Armoured train "Hallerczyk". *The photo was taken in the Polesie region, at the Horodziec railway station in 1920. After the war, the train was disbanded, but the artillery wagon of the* "warsaw" *type, visible in the forefront, remained in service. The locomotive* (G5[4] *Number 4309) had the armour removed and was assigned to regular commercial service. The last wagon, hardly visible in this image, is an artillery wagon with one turret which was previously built for the train* "Gromobój", *and was left in reserve – later it would be converted into an assault wagon.*

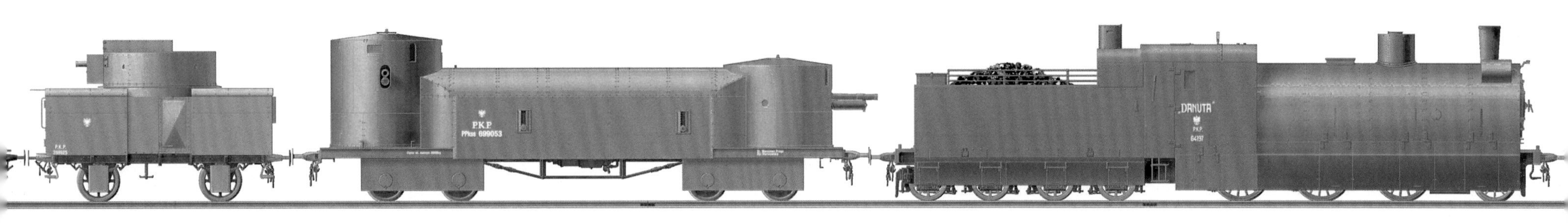
P.K.P
PPkss 699053
„DANUTA"
P.K.P.
64197

HALLERCZYK

When the last of the fighting for borders and independence had ended, the armistice accord with Soviet Russia was put in effect in the autumn of 1920, and the final peace treaty was signed in March of 1921, the authorities could think of a peaceful reorganisation of the troops. However, the peace was not perceived as certain, because it would have been naive to think that Russia ruled by the Bolsheviks, just like the Russia of the Tsars, would abide by any treaties, as long as it decided that it could profit from breaking them. At the end of the war with Soviet Russia in November 1920, the Polish Army had 28 regular armoured trains in service. In accordance with the order of the Chief of the General Staff, in December 1920, the first post-war demobilisation of armoured trains began. It was decided to keep 17 trains in service:

- P.P. 1 **"*Piłsudczyk*"** (ex-Austro-Hungarian, partly new rolling stock from May 1920. In 1921, a part of the older equipment was formed into a separate train, which, together with the volunteers who manned it, became the Silesian insurgent train No. 1 "*Korfanty*");
- P.P. 2 **"*Śmiały*"** (ex-Austro-Hungarian, partly new rolling stock from spring of 1920);
- P.P. 3 **"*Lis-Kula*"** (built in Lwów, new "warsaw" rolling stock from May 1920);
- P.P. 4 **"*Hallerczyk*"** (of the 2nd forming in summer 1920, new "warsaw" rolling stock);
- P.P. 5 **"*Stefan Batory*"** (formed June 1920 in Warsaw, at the front from July 1920);
- P.P. 6 **"*Generał Iwaszkiewicz*"** (of the 2nd forming, October 1920; in 1921 an improvised train was put together from some of the older wagons, and sent to Upper Silesia with a volunteer crew – it was included in the Silesian insurgent armoured train No. 10 "*Ludyga*");

P.P. 4 "Hallerczyk", *composed from brand new rolling stock in the summer of 1920, and decommisioned in Niepołomice in August 1921. From the left: a flat railcar (probably Russian), artillery wagon of the* "warsaw" *type (with anti-aircraft gun wz. 14), Prussian locomotive G5⁴ Number 4309, infantry wagon 11626, artillery wagon from Nowy Sącz built in 1919, already re-armed from an Austrian cannon to a Russian wz. 14 gun (the wagon used, among others, in* "Paderewski" *circa 1919; in the 1930's it was rebuilt into an assault wagon numbered 402633 and assigned to* "Piłsudczyk"*).*

P.P. 7 "*Bolesław Chrobry*" (formed June 1920 in Warsaw, at the front from July 1920);
P.P. 10 "*Pionier*" (built in Lwów, of the 2nd forming);
P.P. 14 "*Zagończyk*" (of the 2nd forming; it was built in Cracow as "*Orzeł Biały*", renamed and reassembled in September 1920);
P.P. 15 "*Paderewski*" (of the 2nd forming 1920, equipped with new "warsaw" type rolling stock);
P.P. 16 "*Mściciel*" (of the 2nd forming, assembled in July 1920);
P.P .20 "*Bartosz Głowacki*" (of the 2nd forming, put together in Cracow in August 1920 from the rolling stock of German armoured trains, sent to the front on 17 August);
P.P. 21 "*Pierwszy Marszałek*" (captured, ex-Soviet *BP No.21* [*BP – bronepoyezd* – armoured train in Russian], converted into the standard-gauge in August 1920);
P.P. 22 "*Groźny*" (of the 3rd forming, captured, ex-Soviet *BP No.56*, changed to standard-gauge from August 1920);
P.P. 23 "*Śmierć*" (formed in Cracow in August 1920);
P.P. 25 "*Stefan Czarniecki*" (built in September 1920 in Nowy Sącz, reserve unit);
P.P. 26 "*Generał Sosnkowski*" (built in Poznań at *Zakłady Cegielskiego* [Cegielski Plant] under construction from August 1920, commissioned on 30 October).

Seven armoured trains were considered to be a mobilisation reserve:

P.P. 8 "*Wilk*" (of the 2nd forming, formed in 1920, "warsaw" rolling stock; some old wagons of this train were used in the 3rd Silesian Uprising);

P.P. 9 "*Danuta*" (of the 2nd forming, new rolling stock);

P.P. 11 "*Poznańczyk*" (of the 2nd forming, new "warsaw" rolling stock);

P.P. 12 "Kaniów" (of the 2nd forming, put together in August 1920);

P.P. 1 "Piłsudczyk" *in September 1920. An artillery wagon with a 122 mm howitzer, built in Lwów, a Series 73.348 locomotive, an assault wagon (the only remnant of the Austro-Hungarian composition captured in Cracow-Prokocim), an improvised infantry wagon and an improvised artillery wagon. A month later, the howitzer wagon was included in the* "Generał Iwaszkiewicz"*. After demobilisation, it was in reserve until the 1930's, when it would be rebuilt and rearmed.*

P.P. 18 "Huragan" *– we are aware of a number of photographs and there are many traces in the archival documents. One of the few trains mobilised in March 1921, in which we are certain of the composition of the rolling stock, as opposed to knowing just the number and name. The train was assembled in August 1920 at Nowy Sącz, and entered combat on 30 August 1920. In December 1920, it left for Poznań, to the* 3. Pułk Wojsk Kolejowych *(3rd Railway Regiment), and was placed in the so called stand-by deposit – with a reduced crew. Some 5 officers, 18 non-commissioned officers and 52 lower ranks would account for roughly half the usual crew. On 15 March 1921, the train became operational again as it was put into combat readiness (it was part of the* V. Dywizjon Pociągów Pancernych, *together with P.P.13* "Zawisza Czarny"*). The demobilisation order followed on 10 June 1921 – the train was finally split up in Poznań in August 1921. In January 1921, the non combat wagons and the officers' passenger carriages of the administrative section were set aside. The combat section's rolling stock at that point was:*

– two artillery wagons built in Cracow on the chassis of Ommku *coal cars, numbers 103227 and 126265, with Austrian 8 cm cannons (previously in the composition of* "Bartosz Głowacki"*).*

– two infantry (assault) wagons: Gg *14200 (armoured in Cracow; previously in the disbanded P.P. 7* "Smok"*) and* Gg *116595.*

– wagon Gr(f) *129862 with a 60 cm searchlight and a field power generator (built in Nowy Sącz in August 1920; the platoon of searchlight operators was sent to its parent battalion in the spring of 1921).*

– two flat railcars, Rm *76761 and* Jke *670866 (with sheet metal covers on the axle grease-boxes).*

– locomotive Series 73.419 with a tender 66.368 (armoured in December 1918 in Lwów as "Lwów II" *train, originally for P.P. 4* "Hallerczyk"*), and the "black" locomotive 73.454 of the administrative supply echelon.*

Gr(f) 129862 wagon with searchlight.

The composition of the "Huragan" *train at the beginning of 1921.*

P.P. 13 "*Zawisza Czarny*" (formed in Lwów, at the front from September 1920);

P.P. 18 "*Huragan*" (constructed at Nowy Sącz in August 1920);

P.P. 24 "*Śmigły*" (captured, ex-Soviet *BP No. 45*, converted into standard-gauge in August 1920).

It was decided to completely disband four armoured trains:

P.P. 17 "*Reduta Ordona*" (put together in Lwów in August 1920, disbanded in Lwów in November 1920, one wagon transferred to the Silesian insurgent train No. 5 "*Powstaniec*" (formerly "*Szwoleżer*");

P.P. 27 "*Ochotnik*" (put together in Stryj in August 1920 as "*Porucznik Kozak*", disbanded December 1920 in Łódź). Several wagons were used in the Silesian armoured train No. 10 "*Ludyga*";

P.P. 27 "*Jan Kiliński*" (ex-Lithuanian No. 1 "*Gediminas*", captured on November 3, 1920, disbanded in November 1920, then reactivated as **P.P . 27 "*Wileńczyk*"**);

P.P. 28 "*General Krajowski*" (ex-*BP No. 39 "Subbotnik"*, captured in Kowel in September 1920).

Earlier, in October 1920, **P.P. 19 "*Podhalanin*"** (broad-gauge – formed temporarily at Sarny in June 1920, changed to a standard-gauge in August) was disbanded.

After the so-called "Rebellion of General Lucjan Żeligowski" and the seizure of Wilno (Vilnius) by Polish troops, a puppet state called Central Lithuania, with Wilno as its capital, was created from part of the Lithuanian territory. Informally dependent on Poland, it remained in existence from 12 October 1920, to 18 April 1922 when it was incorporated with Poland. The state had its own parliament and armed forces, equipped with armoured trains with the following names:

The composition of the "Huragan" train at the beginning of 1921.

"Generał Żeligowski" (ex-P.P. 15 *"Paderewski"*, from 20 October 1920 to August 1921);

"Pogoń" (ex-P.P. 23 *"Śmierć"*, from 7 December 1920).

At the beginning of 1921, it was possible to partially reorganise the armoured trains and put an end to the use of the improvised equipment, whose wartime combat effectiveness and merits were appreciated, but the technical qualities were little or none. Poland already learned how to design and construct "real" combat trains, so it was not necessary to maintain concrete-armoured wagons armed with a random array of guns.

The scheduled demobilisation was interrupted by the events in Upper Silesia, and therefore 24 armoured trains were re-formed with altered combat compositions, from which 12 Armoured Train Groups (*Dywizjon Pociągów Pancernych*) were established. How these trains were

The composition of the "Huragan" train at the beginning of 1921. Locomotive Series 73.419.

composed and which wagons were used we can only surmise. There are just a few documents, and hardly any photographic evidence due to war censorship (in the rare photos released for publication in newspapers, frequent censorship interventions resulted in the rolling stock numbers to be covered or retouched). As the previously ordered demobilisation was well in progress – the re-mobilisation caused quite a chaos – some of the wagons were already disarmed, while some had already been handed over to the *Ministerstwo Kolei Żelaznych* (Ministry of Railways). The composition of the trains that remained in service also changed during this short period of relative calm, as the worn out wagons were temporarily withdrawn. The equipment was undergoing repairs or had new armament fitted. Sometimes, the only thing there was in common with the situation from a few months prior was the name and number of the train retained on paper.

The threat of a war with Germany over the province of Silesia became quite serious. Some of the trains were moved from the east to the vicinity of Upper Silesia – but the frontier with Russia also had to be guarded. The following trains were stationed in Central Lithuania – "*Pierwszy Marszałek*", "*Śmierć*" (a.k.a. "*Pogoń*") and "*Wileńczyk*". Armoured train "*Hallerczyk*" (stationed at Łuniniec) was protecting the border with Soviet Russia, together with "*Groźny*" and "*Śmigły*" (in Kovel). There were "*Stefan Batory*", "*Bolesław Chrobry*" and "*Pionier*" kept in Lwów. There was also "*General Krajowski*" in Równe (in the process of being converted into a standard-gauge). Armoured train "*Śmiały*" was the reserve unit of the High Command of the Polish Army.

Negative political consequences did not allow for any official participation of Polish state in the Third Silesian Uprising – but the use of older improvised armoured wagons converted from commercial railcars (thus easy to conceal) manned by volunteer crews did take place behind the scenes.

Nine improvised armoured trains were delivered from Poland to Silesia – in all, nine armoured locomotives and about 20 wagons. After the uprising, Silesian trains were disbanded – with the exception of the most technologically advanced four:

"*Zygmunt Powstaniec*"
"*Nowak*"
"*Tadek Ślązak*"
"*Piast*"

Opposite page, top: Wagon number Gr 24923 *with a German 77 mm cannon in the Upper Silesian insurgent train* "Ludyga" *taken from the rolling stock of the* "Generał Iwaszkiewicz".

Opposite page, bottom: The Silesian armoured train "Piast".

Right: In both photographs, fragments of the combat section of the Silesian insurgent train "Nowak" *may be seen.*

The insurgent armoured train "Tadek Ślązak".

The trains formally belonged to the Polish Army, and were assigned the *I. Górnośląski Pułk Pociągów Pancernych* (1st Upper Silesian Armoured Train Regiment) stationed in Poznań. This "provisional" unit was not disbanded until 1923.

After the successful plebiscite in Silesia – with the political situation stabilizing – the immediate disbandment of 12 armoured trains began in accordance with the order issued by the Chief of the General Staff on 1 June 1921:

P.P. 3 "*Lis-Kula*" (disbanded in June 1921);
P.P. 4 "*Hallerczyk*" (disbanded August 1921 in Niepołomice);
P.P. 5 "*Stefan Batory*" (disbanded August 1921 in Jabłonna);
P.P. 6 "*Gen. Iwaszkiewicz*" (disbanded September 1921 in Jabłonna);
P.P. 7 "*Bolesław Chrobry*" (disbanded August 1921 in Jabłonna);
P.P. 8 "*Wilk*";
P.P. 10 "*Pionier*" (disbanded in August 1921);
P.P. 12 "*Kaniów*";
P.P. 13 "*Zawisza Czarny*";
P.P. 16 "*Mściciel*" (disbanded at Jabłonna in August 1921);
P.P. 18 "*Huragan*" (in December 1920 kept as a "standby", with a skeleton crew, finally disbanded in Poznań in August 1921);
P.P. 24 "*Śmigły*".

As indicated above, the armoured trains were being decommissioned until as late as August – September of 1921. The train **P.P. 27 "*Wileńczyk*"** stationed in Jabłonna was also disbanded in August 1921.

In July 1921, the rolling stock of the remaining 12 armoured trains was supplemented and strengthened with new types of double-turret artillery wagons; construction process was inaugurated at *Zakłady Cegielskiego* in Poznań towards the end of 1920.

With political tensions looming, it was not until 1923 when it was considered possible for the armed forces to fully switch to peace mode. An order for armoured trains to switch from war readiness to peace mode was issued on 17 October 1923. The railway regiments became places of demobilisation. The combat equipment intended for further service was deposited there, while the unnecessary and redundant wagons and steam locomotives, after disarming and armour removal, were placed at the disposal of the Ministry of Railways.

Twelve trains composed of the most modern and combat worthy equipment were left in service. The twelve remaining armoured trains were divided into six Armoured Train Groups (*Dywizjon Pociągów Pancernych*) of two trains each, and assigned to three railway regiments (*Pułk Saperów Kolejowych*) formed in August 1921: 1st Regiment – Cracow (Niepołomice), 2nd Regiment – Warsaw (Jabłonna), 3rd Regiment – Poznań.

After the regiment from Poznań had been disbanded, the *I.*, *II.*, and *VI. Dywizjon* were transfered to Jabłonna near Warsaw, to the *2. Pułk Saperów Kolejowych* (2nd Railway Engineer Regiment), and the *III.*, *IV.*, and *V. Dywizjon* were incorporated into the *1. Pułk Saperów Kolejowych* (1st Railway Engineer Regiment) in Niepołomice near Cracow.

The Armoured Trains Groups in the new configuration, as well as the individual trains were assembled in a different way – as specified by the order *L.235/Mob.* While maintaining the traditional names, the trains were composed according to

The images on both pages depict the Silesian armoured train "Zygmunt Powstaniec".

the new concepts of operational standards. The individual combat wagon assignments changed from the ones of 1920 and early 1921.

I. Dywizjon Pociągów Pancernych
Armoured Train Number 1 (P.P. 1) "*Danuta*",
Armoured Train Number 2 "*Generał Sosnkowski*".

II. Dywizjon Pociągów Pancernych
Armoured Train Number 3 "*Paderewski*",
Armoured Train Number 4 "*Śmierć*".

III. Dywizjon Pociągów Pancernych
Armoured Train Number 5 "*Śmiały*",
Armoured Train Number 6 "*Groźny*".

IV. Dywizjon Pociągów Pancernych
Armoured Train Number 7 "*Piłsudczyk*",
Armoured Train Number 8 "*Stefan Czarniecki*".

V. Dywizjon Pociągów Pancernych
Armoured Train Number 9 "*I. Marszałek*",
Armoured Train Number 10 "*Bartosz Głowacki*".

VI. Dywizjon Pociągów Pancernych
Armoured Train Number 11 "*Poznańczyk*",
Armoured Train Number 12 "*Zagończyk*".

ARMOURED TRAINS 1924–1929

Opposite page: The military year of 07/I (first draft of the year), that is, the conscripts from 1928 go back to civilian lives. In the background a Tatra *armoured draisine can be seen, on the right – "*Śmiały*" and a locomotive with a tender of unknown type. The barrels of 122 mm* wz. *09 howitzers and 3-inch guns in the turrets are visible in the background.*

The trains arranged according to the new roster from the end of 1923 constituted a mobilisation reserve.

In 1924, the *Dywizjon Ćwiczebny Pociągów Pancernych* (Exercise Group of Armoured Trains) was formed. It was stationed at Jabłonna, formally as the *4. batalion, 2. Pułk Wojsk Kolejowych* (4th Battalion, 2nd Railway Regiment). The group was assigned two trains from the now disbanded *I. Dywizjon* – "*Danuta*" and "*Generał Sosnkowski*", or more precisely – the rolling stock of these trains was utilized. For exercise purposes, wagons from either one of the trains were often coupled together, probably depending on the training requirements. At the beginning of January 1925, the *Dywizjon Ćwiczebny* was renamed the *Dywizjon Szkolny Pociągów Pancernych* (School Group of Armoured Trains), which, as before, was stationed in Jabłonna, but was using a third train – "*Paderewski*", from the dispersed *II. Dywizjon*. The remaining trains stored at Jabłonna and Niepołomice still constituted a mobilisation reserve, which does not mean that they remained idle on the tracks and rusted away. Improvements were continually carried out, routine maintenance was performed, and the equipment was occasionally sent on the move – as in sauntering exercises. The entire rolling stock was also subject to periodic inspections in accordance with the regulations of *P.K.P. (Polskie Koleje Państwowe* – Polish National Railways), which was a required "permit" to participate in railway traffic.

In October 1927, the former *Dywizjon Szkolny* was transformed into the *1. Dywizjon Pociągów Pancernych* (1st Armoured Train Group), and in the spring of 1928 in Niepołomice near Cracow, the *2. Dywizjon Pociągów Pancernych* (2nd Armoured Train Group) was formed. The combat equipment deposited in the railway regiments was transferred to the new formations.

Poligon Ćwiczebny *(Training Ground) of the* 1. Pułk Saperów Kolejowych *(1st Railway Engineer Regiment) in the Grzegórzki district of Cracow, 1927. Sappers (pioneers) are laying a narrow track line (ex-German field design) on a training bridgehead. On the right side wagons from the mobilisation reserve standing next to the shed may be noted – a part of an artillery wagon (later rebuilt into assault wagon 631550 in the* "Groźny" *composition), then an assault wagon 430043, and last artillery wagon 630727 (later with a 100 mm howitzer).*

In December 1929, it was decided to disband one train in the *2. Dywizjon* – "*Stefan Czarniecki*", and another in the *1. Dywizjon* – "*Zagończyk*". The rolling stock of these trains, in conjunction with the reserve equipment (including some of the wagons previously classified as non-standard ones), was intended to create a new, uniform configuration of combat units – five in Legionowo and five in Niepołomice. The extent of equipment exchange between the groups was left to the discretion of unit commanders, but consultation with the commanding officers of respective railway regiments was required.The reorganisation and streamlining activities were basically completed in 1925. After the exclusion of the three trains assigned to the *Dywizjon Ćwiczebny*, the rest of the rolling stock was again placed in mobilisation reserve. Most of the artillery wagons already had their armament replaced and unified – the Austrian and German guns, were switched with the Russian 76.2 mm *wz. 02* cannons and 122 mm howitzers *wz. 09*. In the second half of the 1920s, another change in weaponry began, with the introduction of the *wz. 02/26* cannons (Russian Putilov field guns re-bored and adapted to fire French designed 75 mm ammunition rounds) and 100 mm howitzers *wz. 14/19A*, replacing the Russian 122 mm howitzers (for which the stockpile of ammunition was running low). In the late 1920s, the artillery wagons were fitted with normalized anti-aircraft machine gun turrets. In December 1926, a decision was made to standardise the steam locomotive type; the process began in 1927.

P.P. 1 *"Danuta"* Armoured Train

Armoured Train Number 1 "*Danuta*" was part of the *I. Dywizjon Pociągów Pancernych* (Jabłonna). The second train in the group was P.P. 2 "*Generał Sosnkowski*". From 1924, both trains were assigned to the training unit – *Dywizjon Ćwiczebny Pociągów Pancernych*. In 1925, the unit was reorganised and transformed into *Dywizjon Szkolny Pociągów Pancernych* – with a third train added – P.P. 3 "*Paderewski*".

Locomotive

In 1925, the P.P. 1 "*Danuta*" train had the *G5²* armoured locomotive number 4197 (its designation from the former Prussian railways, after the introduction of the Polish terminology – the lettering and the number scheme – was changed to *Ti2-73*). It was a steam locomotive from the so-called G5 (*Guterzuglokomotive Gruppe 5*), Series 2.

The "*Danuta*" steam locomotive was operational in 1925. It was intended to install an expulsory pump, a type of suction pump using the steam of the locomotive to create vacuum, which would enable refilling of water from random ponds, rivers or even ditches in the event of – for example – the destruction of railway water towers. The attempt was a result of the experiences from the recent war, when there were often problems with filling boilers with water. It was also decided to keep only the steam locomotives with 12 and 16 cubic metre tenders in service, thus discarding all tank engines. Combat actions in the vast areas of eastern borderlands, required the largest possible supply of coal and water.

The collision of "Danuta" *and* "Generał Sosnkowski" *in September 1924 near Olkienniki. In the foreground, the derailed locomotive of the* "Danuta" *–* G5² *Number 4197. In January 1925 the locomotive was rebuild at the railway workshops in Łapy.*

Crew of the P.P.1 "Danuta".

Artillery wagon of the "Danuta" *coupled with artillery wagon 699054 of* "Generał Sosnkowski" *(seen from its higher turret's side). In this commemorative photograph are infantry officer cadets after a training course in cooperation with armoured units. Approximately in 1927. In the inset photograph above: crew of the P.P.1* "Danuta".

A group of conscripts before return to civilian life – commemorative photograph next to the "Danuta" *armoured train. Probably in 1928.*

P.P. 1 "Danuta" *assembled for travel march – Mława, 10.15 hrs., 27 March 1926. The locomotive, positioned in the front, is probably the Ti3-2 (typically serving* "Generał Sosnkowski" *– it is indicated by the silhouette features and very dark paint scheme), followed by both artillery wagons, an assault wagon with a characteristic searchlight turret, and a wagon, quite large, which cannot be clearly identified but could be a freight one.*

„OSA”
NUTA
PKP

Opposite page: Non-commissioned officers by the Tatra *armoured draisine nicknamed* "Osa" *("Wasp"), and the* G5²-4197 "Danuta" *locomotive – during exercises in Rembertów near Warsaw, 29 August 1929.*

"Danuta" *in the 1920's. The American type control flat railcar (four-axle, low-sided), artillery wagon (the number cannot be read), the locomotive from* "Generał Sosnkowski", *second artillery wagon, assault wagon and a second flat railcar, also an American four-axle one (probably with stanchions fitted).*

Profile of the locomotive G5²-4197 *with four-axle tender of the* 16C1 *type.*

Artillery wagons

The train consisted of two identical four-axle artillery wagons 699049 and 699050 (each armed with a Russian 3-inch gun (*wz. 02*, 76.2 mm) and a Russian 48-line howitzer (*wz. 09*, 122 mm). These were wagons developed in 1920 by the Poznań branch of the *Kierownictwo Budowy Pociągów Pancernych* (Armoured Train Construction Directorate), they were referred to as Type II. German flat railcars for rail transport were used – the *SS* type *A3* (*Vierachsiger Schienenwagen*), with a capacity of 35 tons (with a brakeman's cab; overall length of the wagon – 17.1 m; frame length – 15.8 m, bogie spacing – 10 m). Four such wagons were put into service in the first half of 1921 at the HCP Plant in Poznań (*Hipolit Cegielski Towarzystwo Akcyjne*) – out of which two wagons 699051 and 699052, went to the "*Poznańczyk*", replacing the earlier two-axle single-turret wagons in its combat section. In December 1928 it was recommended to repaint the wagons 699049 and 699050 as they appeared "too grey" (the spotted camouflage pattern of 1921was replaced with overall grey in 1924).

A cropped and enlarged fragment of a photograph with artillery wagon PPkss 699050. *In the later military documents, the designations of the type of the wagons' chassis would not be recorded.*

Assault wagon

In 1925 this was the two-axle wagon number 430046 – one of the modern combat wagons build around 1919. After final reorganization of 1930 it was replaced with 423627. In the beginning of 1939 the 430046 wagon was listed in the registers as "in need of repairs" in the *2. Dywizjon*.

In the period of 1921–1924, the steam locomotive and combat wagons underwent a major overhaul, refurbishment and modernizations. During the renovation, automatic brakes were installed; signal lights, bells and audio connections (voice tubes) were also added. In 1925, it was decided to install control lamps in the wagons, which was soon carried out. The wireless communication compartment (designed and fabricated by the *Polskie Towarzystwo Radjotechniczne* [Polish Radio Engineering Society]) in the assault wagon also remained on the list of modifications to be done. Auxiliary accumulator batteries were added to the locomotive accessories.

P.P. 2 *"Generał Sosnkowski"* Armoured Train

Armoured Train Number 2 "*Generał Sosnkowski*" was part of the *I. Dywizjon Pociągów Pancernych* (Jabłonna). The other train in this unit was the P.P. 1 "Danuta". From 1924, both trains were assigned to the *Dywizjon Ćwiczebny* (training unit).

A newspaper image of the "Generał Sosnkowski" *from the autumn of 1920 – the artillery pieces of the train are the original German 77 mm guns. The black spots on the wagons and locomotive are markings and numbers of the rolling stock covered by the censor bars requested by the military.*

Another newspaper photograph using the halftone technique from autum 1920.

And yet another image from a daily paper of autumn 1920 (still with German guns).

Locomotive

The combat section of "*Generał Sosnkowski*" had an armoured steam locomotive Group G5 series 3 – *G5*^{3} with German number 4024 (Polish designation *Ti3*, number 2). There was an intent to install an expulsory pump.

This steam locomotive remained as an allotment engine of the "*Generał Sosnkowski*" until the new composition of armoured trains was introduced in 1930. Afterwards it was transferred to the *2. Dywizjon* and became the standard locomotive of the "*Marszałek*" armoured train.

A cropped and enlarged section of the photograph – Ti3-2 locomotive pulling armoured train "Poznańczyk".

Lower photo opposite page: A training armoured train on the move – a mixed composition: Ti3-2 steam locomotive of the "Generał Sosnkowski", an assault wagon 02019 (usually with "Generał Sosnkowski"), assault wagon 425627 (assigned to "Śmierć") and artillery wagon 450012 (usually incleded in "Paderewski").

The Ti3-2 locomotive in the 1920's.

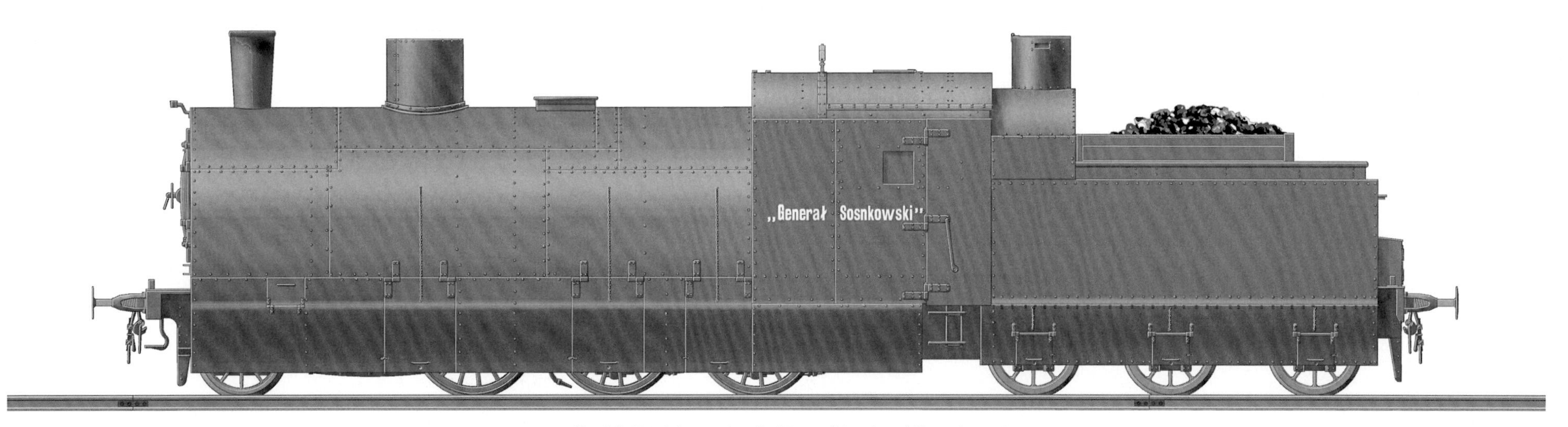

A profile of the Ti3-2 *locomotive, the* "Generał Sosnkowski" *regular engine.*

Artillery wagon number 699054 damaged during the accident at Olkienniki.

Profile of the 398625 wagon.

Artillery wagons

The train had a four-axle artillery wagon 699054 with two Russian 3-inch guns (*wz. 02*, 76.2 mm), which replaced the originally installed German 77 mm *wz. 16* artillery pieces. It was one of the two modern wagons, with guns mounted in cylindrical rotating turrets, of the so-called Type I, designed and built in 1920 at *Cegielski* factory. In 1925, during the repairs after a derailing accident, air brakes were installed.

The second artillery wagon of the "*Generał Sosnkowski*" train was a small two-axle wagon number 398625 (old German number 103227 or 126265) already re-armed from an Austrian 8 cm *wz. 1905/08* cannon to a 3-inch (76.2 mm) gun. The wagon served in the composition of P.P. "*Bartosz Głowacki*" during the war with the Bolsheviks. During the mobilisation in the late 1921 it became part of the "*Huragan*" rolling stock (together with an almost identical wagon 398624). The wagon was built in Cracow as a conversion of a typical Prussian *Ommku* coal car (Prussian pattern *IId1* and German "union" *A6* series). The wagon was intended to be fitted with automatic brakes – which was eventually done, but at a latter time.

The early 1920's – artillery wagons of "Generał Sosnkowski" *with Russian guns mounted. The train's assembly before equipment redistribution in 1924.*

Wagon Number 398625 – still in the composition of the "Bartosz Głowacki" *(it was mobilised in March 1921 for the* "Huragan" *train with no major technical changes; repainted – camouflage pattern with different scheme and possibly different colours). Note the turret's nickname* "Maryś".

The 699054 artillery wagon.

The Dywizjon Szkolny *(Training Group) during excercises.* Ppkss 699054 *wagon of the* "Generał Sosnkowski" *coupled with* PPkss 699050 *of the* "Danuta" *artillery wagon.*

Assault wagon

It was two-axle wagon 02019. It belonged to the group of Polish-built wagons, the so-called "warsaw" type. These were artillery and assault wagons with a characteristic semi-barrel shaped armour profile, built on the standard chassis of Russian 1,000-pood (approx. 36,000 lbs) flat railcars.

In 1925, the rolling stock was reconditioned (it was necessary after the accident in which the train was involved in 1924), and the armament was refitted. In 1925 – as an ongoing improvement process, the light and bell installations were added to the locomotive and the twin-turret 699054 artillery wagon. Automatic brakes were also installed. At that time, a control lamps in the assault wagon and installation of batteries in the locomotive remained as items to be done. Adding to the list, the second artillery wagon and the assault wagon were to be equipped with automatic brakes in the near future (the brake installation work was already underway on in the assault wagon in May 1925).

It is not known when the 02019 assault wagon was transferred to the "*Poznańczyk*" train, and assigned number 620651. It is also uncertain when at which point wagon 423502 was converted from the artillery into an assault wagon and added to the composition of the "*Generał Sosnkowski*".

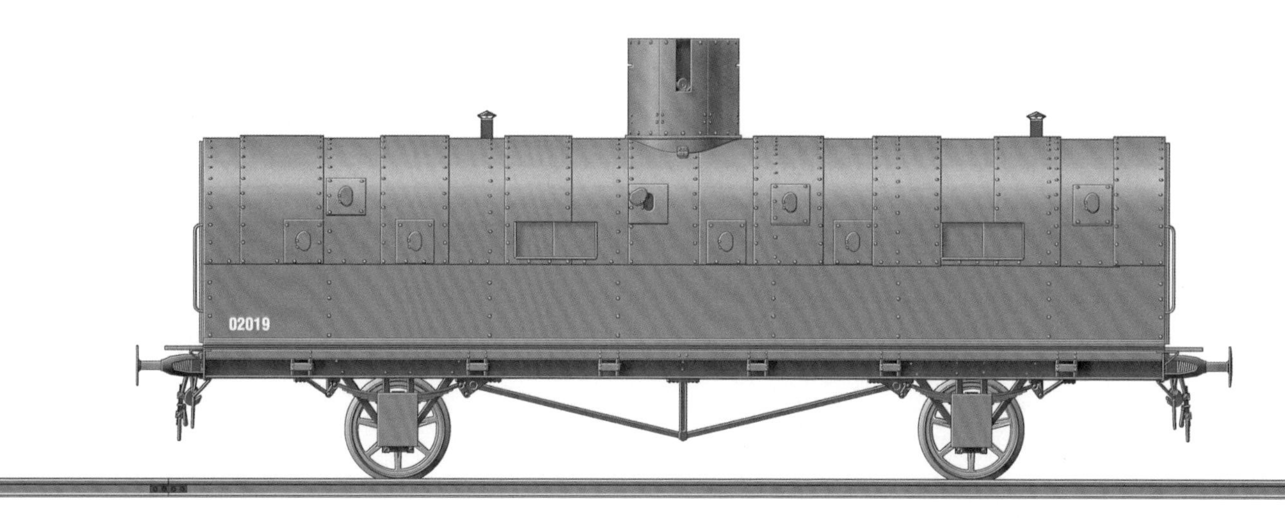

Assault wagon number 02019 of the "Generał Sosnkowski" *train.*

A cropped and enlarged image from 1925 – an assault wagon of the Dywizjon Szkolny.

P.P. 3 *"Paderewski"* Armoured Train

Profile of the G5³-4021 *(Polish number* Ti3-12*) locomotive, the regular engine of the* "Paderewski" *train.*

Armoured Train Number 3 "Paderewski" together with Armoured Train Number 4 "Śmierć" formed the *II. Dywizjon Pociągów Pancernych* (Jabłonna). In 1925, the train was added to the training *Dywizjon Ćwiczebny*.

Locomotive

The train had a Group G5 locomotive, Series 3 – *G5³* number 4021 (Polish designation *Ti3-12*; at an earlier time this locomotive was used in the armoured train P.P. 16 "*Mściciel*", decommissioned in August 1921 in Jabłonna).

The G5³ *number 4021 steam locomotive – photograph from 1920, dating back to the time when the locomotive was pulling the armoured train P.P. 16* "Mściciel", *later disbanded in August 1921 in Jablonna.*

The Dywizjon Szkolny *(Training Group) – exercises in Podbrodzie, 6 August 1925. From the left – an artillery wagon (regular assignment to* "Paderewski"*, still without a number at the time but later designated as 450012), artillery wagon 699054 (from the assembly of* "Generał Sosnkowski"*), assault wagon 02019 (formally assigned to* "Generał Sosnkowski"*)*

Artillery wagon 450012 seen from the end with the 122 mm howitzer turret. There are no additional sheets of armour covering the tubing of the air brakes and it is not possible to see if the observation turret was replaced with a machine gun one. Thus a conclusion that image could be dated back to the late 1920's – it is possible that the photograph was taken after the wagon was handed over to Niepołomice.

Artillery wagons

Armoured train "*Paderewski*" was equipped with two four-axle artillery wagons (without numbers in the 1921–1925 period), each armed with a Russian 3-inch gun (*wz. 02*, 76.2 mm) and a 48-line howitzer (*wz. 09*, 122 mm). At a much later time the wagons were given the numbers 660601 and 450012. In 1925 the wagons were in good condition – the equipment was renovated, the only thing left to do was to install communication lights as well as electric lighting, and to fit automatic brakes (or rather refurbish and reconnect them, because the original chassis of the American-built Drop Bottom Gondola railcars were already equipped with an air installation by the manufacturer). The work was done after the completion of the modifications to the "*Generał Sosnkowski*" rolling stock. The 660601 wagon was not assigned to any of the trains during the 1930 reorganisation and was removed from the records of the *1. Dywizjon* in 1931, but most of the armour was modified and installed onto a different chassis.

Assault wagon

Due to the shortage of modern assault wagons, the train did not have one at that time.

P.P. 4 *"Śmierć"* Armoured Train

Armoured Train Number 4 "*Śmierć*", together with Armoured Train Number 3 "*Paderewski*", was part of the *II. Dywizjon Pociągów Pancernych* (Jabłonna). After disbandment of the *II. Dywizjon* ("*Paderewski*" left for the *Dywizjon Ćwiczebny*) the train remained in mobilisation reserve.

Locomotive

The train had a Group G5 steam locomotive Series 1 – *G5¹* number 4018 (Polish designation *Ti1-26*). It was replaced with a standard *Ti3* (*Ti3-5*) as late as 1931.

Artillery wagons

The train used a four-axle artillery wagon, the so-called Type I, number 699053, with two 3-inch *wz. 02* guns (they replaced previously mounted German 77 mm *wz.16* guns). Weapon condition – was noted as good. The wagon was identical to 699054 from "*Generał Sosnkowski*". The only difference was the absence of the rooftop observation turret equipped with heavy machine gun (limited to ground target fire), and artillery turret construction which was welded rather than riveted. In 1925, during the renovation after the railway accident in 1924, automatic air brakes were installed and electrical signalling fitted. At the end of 1925, what remained was the installation of a control lights system.

A G5¹ locomotive number 4018 of the "Śmierć" *armoured train in September 1920. On the right a part of an assault wagon may be seen; the wagon was later given the number 425627.*

The second wagon was a two-axle artillery wagon 398624 (old German number 103227 or 126265) with a 3-inch gun – coincidentally, almost identical to the wagon 398625 serving in the "*Generał Sosnkowski*". It also belonged to the wartime rolling stock of "*Bartosz Głowacki*" and later "*Huragan*" armoured trains. The armament condition was assessed as good. In 1925, it was decided to install automatic brakes and signal lights.

Assault wagon

The assault wagon was numbered 425627. It was built at the Zieleniewski factory in Cracow on the chassis of a Prussian coal car with a capacity of 20 tons. It was a two-axle wagon with a wheelbase of 4.5 m with brakeman's cab, one of the few modern assault wagons constructed during Polish – Soviet war era. In 1925 the intended changes included armour modification, removal of the cylindrical superstructure and installation of automatic brakes and signal lights. The work was not completed until the mid-1930's. In September 1920 the wagon was assigned to the P.P. 23 "*Śmierć*" (in December 1920, the train – as P.P. 23 "*Pogoń*" – became part of the armed forces of Central Lithuania). The original superstructure housed an Austrian 60 cm field searchlight which was operated by a platoon (actually an officer and four to five

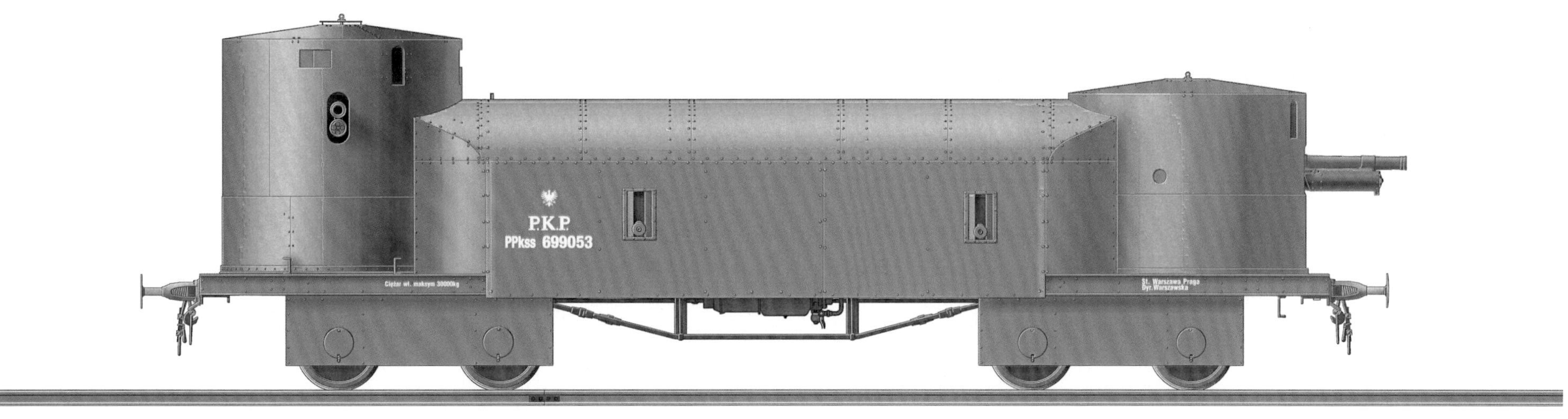

A profile of the 699053 artillery wagon. It is painted overall grey and has the air brake system already fitted.

A cropped fragment of a photo taken at Pilawa in 1931 – artillery wagon 398624 and assault wagon 425627 remain in an unmodified form dating back to 1920's.

man of lower ranks, thus an incomplete squad) of searchlight engineers detached from the *Batalion Maszynowy Saperów* (Machine Engineer Battalion), and eventually sent back to their parent battalion on 21 April 1921 after the searchlight was removed.

A profile of the wagon 425627 – it was rebuilt only in the mid-1930's.

Photograph of "Bartosz Głowacki" *as of August 1920. The wagon on the left is numbered 398625 (after a short episode in the* "Huragan" *in 1921, it finally ended up in the* "Generał Sosnkowski"*); the following one is 398624, which reinforced the rolling stock of the* "Śmierć".

The ceremony of consecrating the train P.P. 23 "Śmierć" *before leaving for the front in August 1920 – the assault wagon was later designated with number 425627.*

P.P. 11 *"Poznańczyk"* Armoured Train

Armoured Train Number 11 "*Poznańczyk*", together with Armoured Train Number 12 "*Zagończyk*", formed the *VI. Dywizjon Pociągów Pancernych* (first at Poznań, then in Jabłonna). It remained in the mobilisation reserve until the reorganization of 1930.

Locomotive

The train had a Group G7 steam locomotive number 4460. The Prussian Series $G7^1$ (designated as Polish *Tp1* type) and Series $G7^2$ (Polish *Tp2* type) were the steam cargo locomotives with the 0-4-0 (OOOO) wheel arrangement. Some 1200 $G7^1$ steam locomotives were built in the period 1893–1917 – in the *P.K.P.* there were 142 of them. There were 295 more G7 Series 2 locomotives (1650 were built between 1895 and 1911).

At a later time the *G7-4460* of "*Poznańczyk*" was replaced, for a short time, with a locomotive the train had already used prior to 1924, a $G5^2$ with German number 4199 (Polish designation *Ti2-74*). The *G7-4460* locomotive was most likely designated as *Tp1-112*. If so, it lasted in service with the armoured train groups until the early 1930s, when it was replaced by a *Ti3-16* steam locomotive.

The *G7-4460* steam locomotive was in good technical condition. The only directive from the period recommends repainting the armour (it was dark grey).

"Poznańczyk" *in the mid 1920's (with a locomotive of the* "Danuta"*).*

The locomotive was not equipped with an air compressor, as at the time it was not intended to install an air brake system on the wagons of P.P. 11 "*Poznańczyk*".

Artillery wagons

In 1925, the train consisted of two four-axle artillery wagons: 699051 and 699052 (the latter initially retained the number of the German flat railcar on which it had been constructed – 322516). Each wagon was armed a 3-inch gun (*wz. 02*, 76.2 mm) and 48-line howitzer (*wz. 09*, 122 mm). The wagons designed in 1920 at the Poznań branch of *Kierownictwo Budowy Pociągów Pancernych* (Armoured Train Construction Directorate), were built using the German *Vierachtsiger Schienennwagen* (four-axle rail carrying) flat railcars. The series consisted of four wagons and was designated as Type II.

Assault wagon

In 1925, the train did not have an assault wagon. It is not possible to determine the date, but at some time a "warsaw" type wagon number 62065 (the former 02019 from "*Generał Sosnkowski*") was assigned to the "*Poznańczyk*" train. By the time of transfer the wagon was already rebuilt – armoured plates covering the undercarriage were added and Westinghouse brakes were installed. The wireless set was fitted relatively early in comparison with other wagons. Initially, the antenna wire stretched between T-shaped half masts, later two oblique half masts, but finally, after the experimental phase was over, some time in the 1930s, an upright set of masts was installed, as in on all other trains.

It was necessary to install the system of signal lamps and bells to match the standard. The wagons had no automatic brakes at that time – they were eventually installed after the full introduction of the standard Ti3 locomotives.

Locomotive G5²-4199 (Polish number Ti2-74). A photograph from 1919, the first combat formation of the "Poznańczyk".

Locomotive G5²-4199 in 1920.

Yet another image of the very same locomotive G5²-4199 in 1920.

An image from a photographic session in 1923 – officers of the "Poznańczyk" *at the artillery wagon, before being transferred to the* VI. Dywizjon *in Jabłonna.*

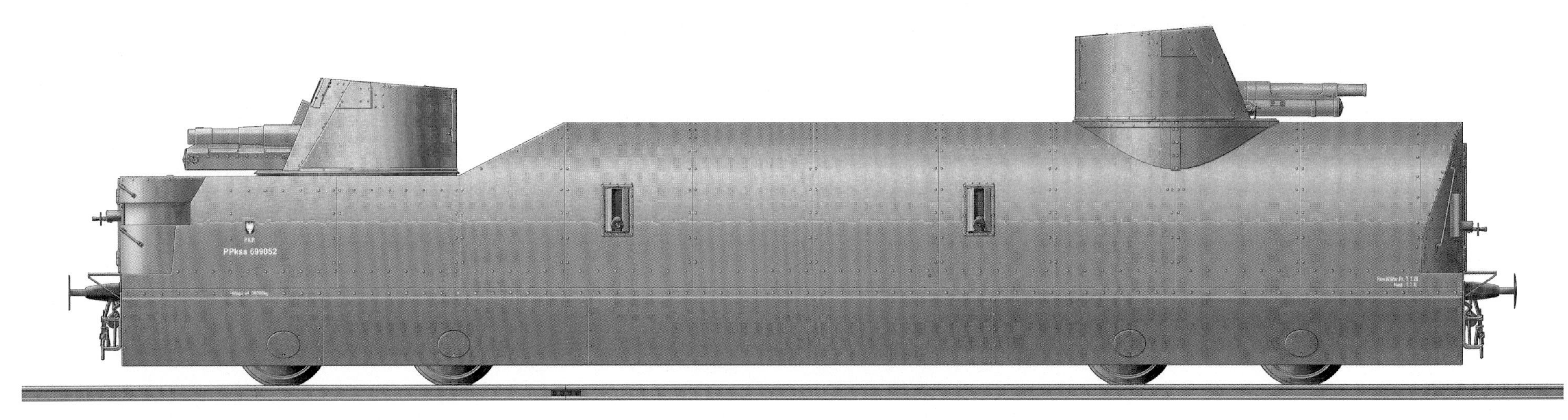

Profile of the artillery wagon 699052 of the "Poznańczyk".

A second surviving photograph of the set taken in taken in 1923 – officers of the "Poznańczyk".

The "mobilisation reserve" activated – "Poznańczyk" *during emergency drill exercises around 1928. It is clearly visible that the drum machine guns mounts are inclined according to the curvature of the side wall armour (the design was later altered for ease of operation).*

Armoured train P.P. 11 "Poznańczyk" in the composition for a combat movement – a Tatra draisine (number 102, called "Żuk" – "Beetle") may be seen at the forefront of the battle configuration of the train: front flat railcar (four-axle, American type), front artillery wagon, $G5^3$ locomotive (number 4024, officially assigned to P.P.2 "Generał Sosnkowski"; according to a method determined later, it should be placed with a tender in the direction of travel), assault wagon, rear artillery wagon. Noteworthy, a rear flat railcar is absent. The second Tatra draisine is in the back of the train. The photo was probably taken in 1928.

Type II artillery wagon. On the right, a part of the assault wagon number 620651 is visible.

Assault wagon of the "Poznańczyk" number 620651. The number prior to modification was 02019 – the changes included the addition of the armoured aprons protecting the chassis and half-masts with the radio antenna cable. Later, further changes were implemented – the machine gun turret was removed, new radio antenna masts were fitted and the full length apron was cut out to protect just the vital components.

P.P. 12 *"Zagończyk"* Armoured Train

Armoured Train Number 12 "*Zagończyk*", together with Armoured Train Number 11 "*Poznańczyk*", formed the *VI. Dywizjon Pociągów Pancernych* (Jabłonna). "*Zagończyk*" remained in the mobilisation reserve until 1929, when it was disbanded.

The $G5^4$ – 4202 locomotive of the "Zagończyk" train was not armoured – "black" in 1925.

Locomotive

In 1925, the combat section had a *$G5^4$* steam locomotive number 4202 (Polish designation was probably *Ti4-13*; later, this steam locomotive served for a short time with the "*Paderewski*" train), with a four-axle tender (most likely). In 1925, the steam locomotive was "black"; its armour was removed since the engine was to be returned to the Ministry of Railways. The intent was to replace it with series *G7* armoured locomotive soon to be delivered from the workshops in Nowy Sącz.

Artillery wagons

The combat section had an unusual composition of three artillery wagons. It contained two ex-Austrian-Hungarian twin-axle artillery wagons – 141455 (war booty from Cracow-Prokocim; assigned to "*Piłsudczyk*" during the war with the Bolsheviks; number later changed to 153650), and 141164 (identical wagon of the same origin, which served with "*Śmiały*" armoured train). There was a third artillery wagon built on the Austrian two-axle flat railcar series *Jke*, number 673023 (previously used, among others, in the composition of "*Gromobój*"). At the time all three wagons were already converted from Austrian cannons to Russian 3-inch guns.

Assault wagon

The assault wagon was identified with number 390243. It was also a captured wagon from the *k.u.k.* Cracow-Prokocim armoured train. It spent the war of 1918 – 1920 with armoured train "*Śmiały*". After the 1924 armoured train accident, the wagon was in need of repair so by 1925 automatic brakes were installed (the coal supply storage boxes under the under-frame had to be removed); the electrical signals were also put in place during the renovation.

Artillery wagon 141164, which had previously served in "Śmiały"*, had already undergone some gun exchanges – after an Austro-Hungarian naval gun, followed by an Austro-Hungarian field gun, a Russian 3-inch cannon was mounted in 1925.*

Artillery wagon 141164 of the "Śmiały" (still with an Austrian 8 cm field cannon), behind it an assault wagon 390243. Photograph taken in 1920.

Artillery wagon with a Russian wz. 02 gun. Much later, probably during the replacement of the wz. 02 gun with a wz. 02/26 gun, the cannon trunnion was moved forward (due to the length of gun recoil) so an armoured sponson had to be added in the front.

Artillery wagon 141164 in the "Śmiały" (spring 1919, Cracow).

Artillery wagon 141455 previously used in the "Piłsudczyk" (image from 1919).

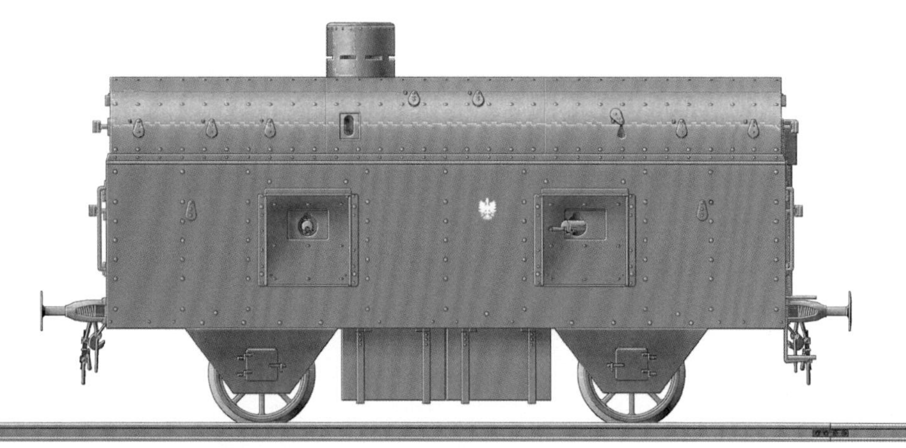

A profile of the 390243 assault wagon before it had its air brakes fitted.

An artillery wagon of the "Piłsudczyk" *seen in a photograph taken in 1918.*

In the background of this commemorative photograph taken in June 1919, the sliding door in the open position at the back of the gun turret is visible.

The artillery wagon number 141455 of the "Piłsudczyk" *armoured train.*

The 390243 assault wagon in the combat section of the "Śmiały" *– cropped and enlarged image from a photograph taken in the spring of 1920.*

P.P. 5 *"Śmiały"* Armoured Train

The *Dywizjon Pociągów Pancernych Numer III* (3rd Armoured Trains Group) – Niepołomice included the Armoured Train Number 5 "*Śmiały*" and the Armoured Train Number 6 "*Groźny*". They remained in the mobilisation reserve until introduction of the new train assignment in 1930.

Locomotive

The train retained its original Prussian Series *G5⁴* armoured locomotive number 4321 (Polish designation *Ti4* number 180). *Polskie Koleje Państwowe* (Polish State Railways) acquired over 200 *G5⁴* locomotives. After the introduction of Polish nomenclature, they received the designation *Ti4*. During the border wars, seven locomotives of this group were armoured – they served with "*Paderewski*", "*Bolesław Chrobry*", "*Hallerczyk*" and "*Śmiały*" trains, among others. The *Ti4-180* locomotive was eventually replaced by the *Ti3-4* locomotive in 1931.

Artillery wagons

The train had two four-axle artillery wagons of identical construction. These were: wagon number 699020, stationed at Legionowo at the time the armoured trains groups were formed, and transferred to the armoury in Kraków, where it was included in the "*Śmiały*" train, and wagon number 699021. The wagons were of Polish construction from the Cegielski Plant in Poznań; known as Type III. Each of them had a Russian 3-inch gun (76.2 mm, *wz. 02*) and a Russian 48-line howitzer (122 mm, *wz. 09*) in rotating turrets. For a brief time after construction, the wagons retained the numbers of the German *Vierachsiger Schienenwagen* flat railcars, on which the armoured bodies had been mounted – 35463 and 322647.

Assault wagon

In 1925, "*Śmiały*" did not have an assault wagon. It was not until 1929, when wagon 627950 was assigned to the train.

The permanent cadre of non-commissioned officers of the "Śmiały", *taken in approximately 1929.*

Armoured train crew at the 122 mm howitzer turret of the "Śmiały" *train.*

A "flag gala" during The Soldier's Day – a holiday established to commemorate the victory over the Bolsheviks. New rolling stock of the "Śmiały", 15 August 1921.

Another view of the “Śmiały” *in 15 August 1921.*

P.P. 6 *"Groźny"* Armoured Train

The *Dywizjon Pociągów Pancernych Numer III* (Niepołomice) consisted of Armoured Train Number 6 "*Groźny*" and Armoured Train Number 5 "*Śmiały*". The train remained in mobilisation reserve until the reorganization of 1930.

Locomotive

"*Groźny*" had a Prussian series $G5^2$ steam locomotive number 4153 (later Polish designation *Ti2* number 2). After the war, *P.K.P.* took over 82 locomotives of this type. They were largely worn out – by 1939 little more than 40 survived in service. At least four $G5^2$ steam locomotives were armoured – they were used, by "*Marszałek*", "*Danuta*" and "*Poznańczyk*".

The $G5^2$ steam locomotive No. 4153 originally came from the wartime composition of the "*Marszałek*", in which it replaced the Russian O^W series locomotive after the rolling stock had been converted into standard-gauge. In 1925, it was decided to install batteries in the locomotive and fit voice and internal signal light systems.

The ex-Bolshevik BP (bronyepoyezd – *armoured train)* "Kommunar" *artillery wagon in the composition of the* "Groźny-szeroki" *(*szeroki – *broad-gauge).*

The same ex- Kommunar wagon in March 1920 of "Groźny-szeroki"*– Converted into standard-gauge in September 1920.*

Artillery wagons

The train had a four-axle artillery wagon number 460024 improvised from an American coal car with a 3-inch gun in a cylindrical turret at one end. It was built by the Bolsheviks in August 1919 as a wagon for the *BP No. 104 "Imeni Karla Libknechta"*. It had the original number 928986 and carried the name *"Ukraina"*. After capture it supplemented the composition of the broad-gauge train P.P. 22 "*Groźny*", also referred to "*Groźny-szeroki*" (*szeroki* – broad). In 1930 the complete lack of mobilisation capability was recorded (the wagon was armoured with rails fitted in the interior and the turret had only 5 mm thick armour plates).

The second artillery wagon was a four-axle wagon number 460025 with two turrets armed with 3-inch guns. It was also a war booty captured from the Bolsheviks – a wagon of the *BP No. 56 "Kommunar"* train seized in March 1920. In September 1920, the "*Groźny-szeroki*" train was moved to Dęblin (to the extent of which the broad-gauge tracks reached) to retrofit it with the standard-gauge wheel bogies.

An ex "Kommunar" *wagon photographed with a former Russian "half-armoured"* O[W] *series locomotive, spring 1920.*

Assault wagon

The assault wagon was numbered 02009 and was a modern assault wagon of Polish construction; it belonged to the so-called "warsaw" – built type with a semi-barrel shape of the armoured body. Its number was still the original designation of the Russian flat railcar chassis, and what became the Polish designation *P.K.P.* number could not be unequivocally established.

The wagon was to be modernised with the installation of automatic brakes (the artillery wagons of the train, 460025 and 460024, on the American-manufactured Drop Bottom Gondola chassis, already had air installations).

What was planned to do was to upgrade the internal signalling devices, that is, to install the electrical lamps, signal bells and the fitting of voice tubes.

A wagon named "Ukraina" *from the former Soviet* "Imeni Karla Libknechta" *armoured train in August 1919.*

An extremely interesting, but regrettably damaged, photograph of the "Groźny-szeroki".

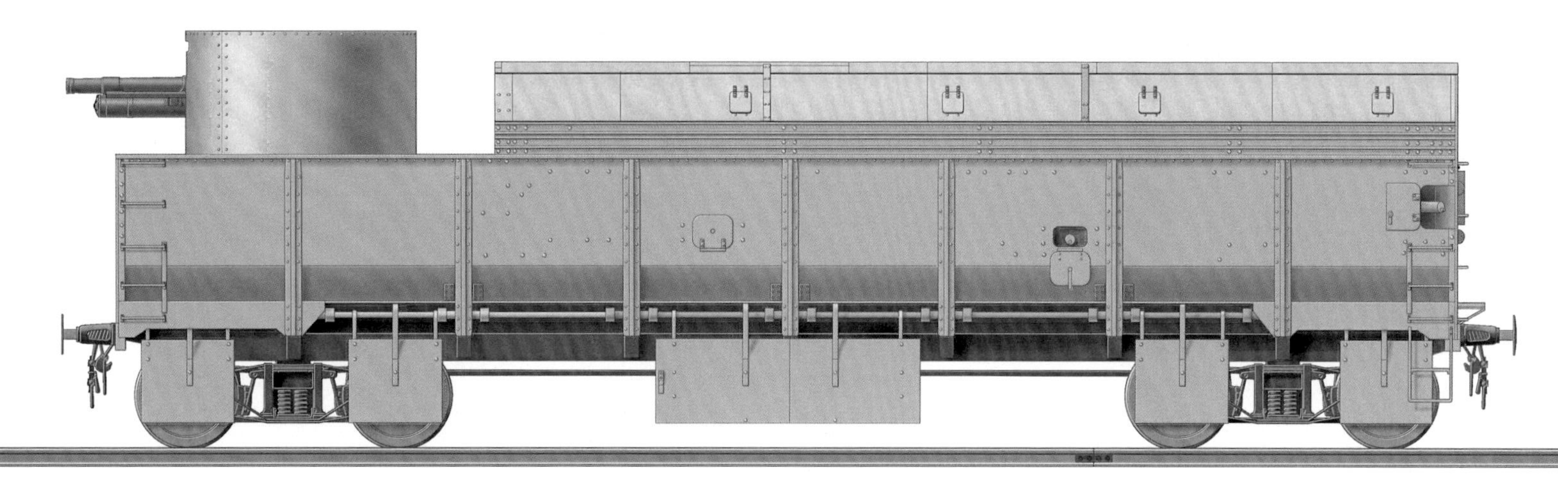

A profile of wagon number 460024 of the "Groźny".

The 460024 artillery wagon in the combat section of the "Groźny".

P.P. 7 *"Piłsudczyk"* Armoured Train

The *Dywizjon Pociagów Pancernych Numer IV* (Niepołomice) included Armoured Train Number 7 "*Piłsudczyk*" and Armoured Train Number 8 "*Stefan Czarniecki*". In the mobilisation reserve until the new organization was introduced in 1930.

Locomotive

The train did not have an assigned locomotive at that time. In the event of mobilisation, the *DOKP – Dyrekcja Okręgowa Kolei Państwowych* (Regional Directorate of the State Railways) was to re-armour cargo locomotive *$G7^{1}$* number 4408. The locomotive was used in civilian service by *P.K.P.* in the district of Cracow and the armour was deposited at the local railway workshop. back in the days of service as an armoured steam locomotive, it used to power "*Zagończyk*" armoured train. The later Polish designation was *Tp1* with the uncertain number, perhaps 112. The probability is low as number 112 is listed in a document from May 1931 in which the *Ti1-112* armoured locomotive was part of the rolling stock of the *1. Dywizjon.*

Artillery wagons

The train had two Polish-built artillery wagons, both of the same Type III from the Cegielski Plant as the wagons of "*Śmiały*" – with a 3-inch gun (*wz. 02*, 76.2 mm) and a 48-line howitzer (*wz. 09*, 122 mm). The wagons had *P.K.P.* numbers 699069 and 699070.

Assault wagon

The train did not have its own assault wagon in 1925.

Workers of the Cegielski Plant, 1921. "Piłsudczyk" *can be seen in the background.*

"Piłsudczyk"– *the crew and the flag gala. The Soldier's Day, 15 August 1921.*

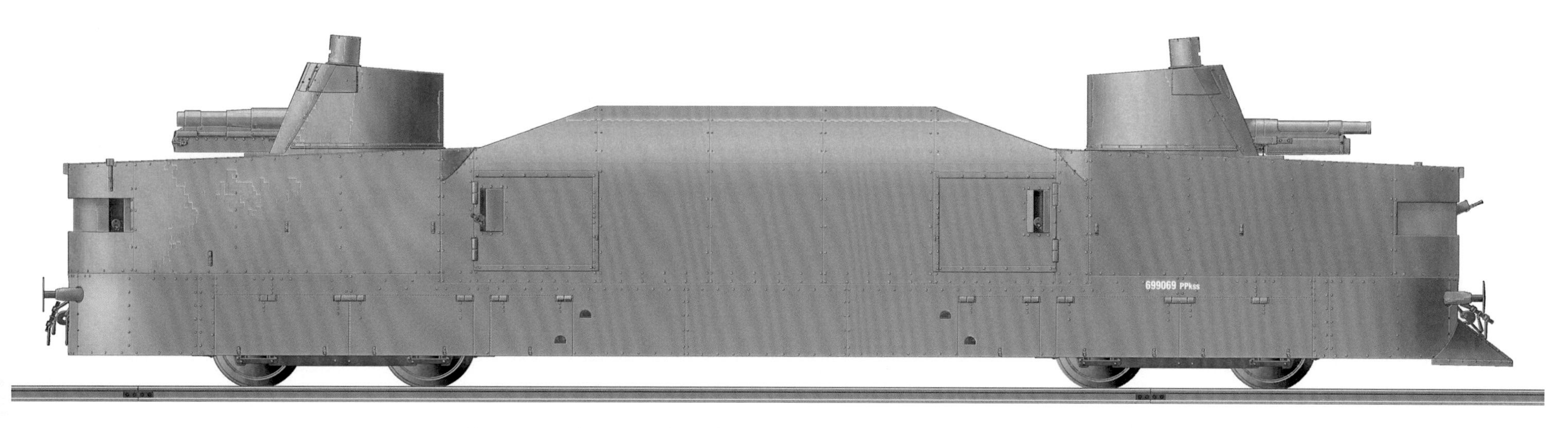

Artillery wagon number 699069 of the "Piłsudczyk" approximately in 1924, already painted overall grey.

The "Piłsudczyk" artillery wagon, 1921.

"Piłsudczyk" in 1922 artillery wagon number 6999069. The original number of the German flat railcar is still visible painted just below the Polish P.K.P. number, but cannot be unequivocally deciphered.

P.P. 8 *"Stefan Czarniecki"* Armoured Train

The *Dywizjon Pociągów Pancernych Numer IV* (Niepołomice) consisted of Armoured Train Number 7 "*Piłsudczyk*" and Armoured Train Number 8 "*Stefan Czarniecki*". The "*Stefan Czarniecki*" remained in the mobilisation reserve until 1929, when it was decommissioned.

Locomotive

In 1925, "*Stefan Czarniecki*", just like "*Piłsudczyk*", did not have a permanently assigned armoured locomotive in its composition. In the event of the mobilisation announcement, it was to receive a re-armoured Prussian steam locomotive series *G7* number 5842. The armour was deposited at the railway workshops in Cracow, and the locomotive was in every-day use at the *DOKP Kraków.*

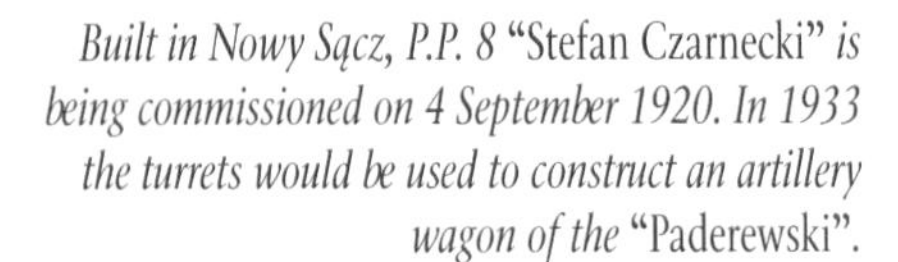

Built in Nowy Sącz, P.P. 8 "Stefan Czarnecki" *is being commissioned on 4 September 1920. In 1933 the turrets would be used to construct an artillery wagon of the* "Paderewski".

Artillery wagons

The train had a two-axle artillery wagon number 658126, of Polish design built at Nowy Sącz, armed with two Austrian 8 cm cannons, and a two-axle Polish artillery wagon number 430044 with one Austrian 8 cm cannon. The artillery wagons were to be retrofitted with Russian guns in the near future, and it is possible that this was done before the later conversion of both into the four axle artillery wagon and an assault wagon respectively – it is however, uncertain. Internal signal installations were also to be completed. Some time later, the 430044 wagon was converted into an assault wagon and at the end of the 1920s it was assigned to the *2. Dywizjon*.

An assault wagon of the original "Piłsudczyk" *composition which would become part of the* "Stefan Czarnecki" *rolling stock.*

To the right and below: An artillery wagon armed with an Austrian 8 cm cannon. It had the number 430044, and was later converted into an assault wagon.

Assault wagon

Assault wagon number 140866 (Austrian number – later Polish number was 393088) was part of the booty from Cracow-Prokocim. As part of the modification program, the internal signal installations were to be fitted.

P.P. 9 *"I. Marszałek"* Armoured Train

It was also listed as "*I-Marszałek*", "*Pierwszy Marszałek*" and, for short, simply "*Marszałek*". The train alongside the Armoured Train Number 10 "*Bartosz Głowacki*" formed the *Dywizjon Pociągów Pancernych Numer V* (Niepołomice). The train was in the mobilisation reserve until the new organization of 1930.

Locomotive

In mid-1925, the train still had the ex-Austrian locomotive Series 73 with the number 86 (Polish series designation *Tp15*, the number could not be determined). At that time, there were 207 of these locomotives in the service of the *P.K.P.* (Polish State Railways). The locomotive was armoured at the L. Zieleniewski works. During the Polish-Soviet War, this locomotive served in the P.P. 22 "*Groźny*" (of the 3rd forming). The locomotive was to be dis-armoured and handed over to the *DOKP Kraków* for regular civilian use after the Nowy Sącz plant had provided a replacement armoured locomotive series *G7*. The armour of the locomotive 73.86 was to be deposited at the *Centralny Zarząd Parków i Warsztatów Saperów Kolejowych* (Central Management of (machine) Parks and Workshops of Railway Engineers), as it was stated: "in an immutable complete set" – clearly, possible future use was envisioned.

In both images: The Soviet BP No. 21 "Imeni Shaumian i Japaridze" *– a war loot photographed on 27 April 1920.*

The "Strzelec Kresowy 13. Dywizji Piechoty" *(The Eastern Borderland Rifleman of the 13th Infantry Division) was formally commissioned under the name of the first Polish military marshal* – "Pierwszy Marszałek".

A standard-gauge locomotive, ex-Austrian, Series 73 number 86 (originally of the 3rd forming of the "Groźny") was assigned to "Pierwszy Marszałek" after the train was converted to standard-gauge in 1920 at Dęblin.

Series 73 locomotives were cargo locomotives with the 0-4-0 (OOOO) wheel configuration. The withdrawal of this type of locomotive from service in armoured trains was entirely justified, because the performance was not the best, and the very unstable behaviour on the move meant that it was necessary to limit its top speed to 35 km/h. Armoured steam locomotives, weighted down with steel plates, behaved slightly better, but they were abandoned anyway. In the civilian service, Series 73 was most often used in shunting service because the engines handled well only at low speeds.

The planned delivery of the *G7* locomotive never actually took place, because in the following year – 1926, a decision was made to standardise steam locomotives in all railway troops (including armoured train units), and the selected standard was the Prussian Series *G5³*, designated by *P.K.P.* as *Ti3* locomotives.

Artillery wagons

The train had a four-axle artillery wagon No. 460023 with two 3-inch guns (the so-called "*Sormovo*" type built at the *Krasnoye Sormovo* plant in Nizhny Novgorod). It was war booty from the Bolsheviks – one of two identical wagons of the *BP No. 21* train "*Imeni Shaumiana i Japaridze*."

The second artillery wagon was an older two-axle wagon number 430023 with one 3-inch gun (*wz. 02*, 76.2 mm).

Assault wagon

The train was not assigned an assault wagon.

"Pierwszy Marszałek" *in the autumn of 1920.*

Officers and subordinate ranks of the "Pierwszy Marszałek", *March 1924.*

„PIERWSZY „MARSZAŁEK"

P.P. 10 *"Bartosz Głowacki"* Armoured Train

Armoured Train Number 10 "*Bartosz Głowacki*" (also listed as "*B. Głowacki*") and Armoured P.P. 9 "*Marszałek*" together formed the *Dywizjon Pociągów Pancernych Numer V* (Niepołomice). They remained in the mobilisation reserve until the introduction of the new organizational structure in 1930.

Locomotive

Just like "*Marszałek*", "*Bartosz Głowacki*" train had an ex-Austrian locomotive – an engine of the 73 series, number 376. It was a locomotive armoured back in May 1919. For some time it was used with the train P.P. 18 "*Odsiecz II*" (after it had been manned by the crew of the destroyed broad-gauge train "*Generał Iwaszkiewicz*" in July 1920, the train was renamed as P.P. 6 "*Generał Iwaszkiewicz*"). It was intended to remove the armour and transfer the locomotive to the civilian service (which was eventually accomplished; the engine served with the *P.K.P.* as *Tp15-177*). Its place was to be taken by a *G7* locomotive from Nowy Sącz.

A 73.376 locomotive in October 1920, still in the composition of the "Generał Iwaszkiewicz".

A profile of the Series 73 number 376 steam locomotive.

Artillery wagons

The train had a captured "*Sormovo*" type artillery wagon with two Russian 3-inch guns (identical to the one in "*Marszałek*") with the Number 460022 – also from the captured Bolshevik train *BP No. 21* "*Imeni Shaumiana i Japaridze*". The second artillery wagon was a two-axle 3-inch gun wagon – number 673025 (or possibly 673023?).

Assault wagon

In 1925, the train was not assigned an assault wagon.

"Bartosz Glowacki" *in Upper Silesia, summer 1921. The artillery and assault wagons served previously in the* "Lis-Kula" *(a.k.a.* "Pepetrójka"*) armoured train, which was disbanded in June 1921. When a new train composition was introduced in 1924, the artillery wagon remained with the* "Bartosz Głowacki", *while the assault wagon was most likely scrapped for unknown reasons.*

Rolling stock reserve

The reserve equipment deposited at Jabłonna, in the *2. Pułk Saperów Kolejowych* (2nd Railway Engineer Regiment), consisted of artillery wagons with the numbers 426048 and 426049 (it can be assumed that these were the wagons of former "*Poznańczyk*" composition before the train was equipped with modern Type II wagons), the 430045 (already with Russian 3-inch guns, in the process of re-arming since 1925) and wagon number 430047 with the Russian 48-line howitzer – in needed of repair (the original number was 248193). The overall assessment mentioned good mechanical condition of the wagons.

The reserve remaining at the disposal of the *1. Pułk Saperów Kolejowych* in Cracow in 1925 consisted of four artillery wagons – two-axle, number 02029 of the "warsaw" type, with a 3-inch Lender gun (new number 630728 or 630729 [archival document is blurry]) and three wagons with Austrian 8 cm cannons – number 423502 (from the wartime rolling stock of "*Paderewski*" and later "*Hallerczyk*") which was eventually converted into an assault wagon after the removal of the turret, and later transferred to Legionowo, without the number change). Wagon 02021 of "warsaw" type, also converted into an assault wagon (casemate armour was extended to replace the dismantled turret) and assigned new number 630726). Lastly, 02006 artillery wagon, again "warsaw"-built, later re-armed with

Bottom: The "warsaw" *type artillery wagon 02006 – in October 1920 it served with the* "Reduta Ordona" *train, and earlier with the* "Lis-Kula"*. Once it had been re-armed with a 100 mm howitzer, it was numbered 630727.*

Wagon 430043 of the "Stefan Czarnecki" *train in September 1920. It was armoured with 12 mm thick plates, and a 10 cm thick layer of concrete poured into a framework; the top was covered with a 3-5 mm sheets of metal. Not too extensively rebuilt, in September 1939 it was a reserve wagon of the* Ośrodek Zapasowy Pociągów Pancernych *(Reserve Detachment of the 2nd Armoured Train Group).*

Above: P.P. 11 "Poznańczyk" in 1920 – from the old composition; the wagons were eventual replaced with the modern Type II from the Cegielski Plant. The old artillery wagons were kept as surplus equipment.

The "lwów" type artillery wagon equipped with 122 mm howitzer and numbered 238193; for some time it remained in reserve, but was later extensively modified and re-armed with a 100 mm howitzer (new number assignment – 430047). In September 1939 it went off to battle as a part of the "Śmierć" armoured train.

a 100 mm howitzer, with a new number 630727.

Apart from the combat wagons, which were listed on the roster as reserve surplus, there were still several, at least a dozen, additional wagons left to be disassembled for possible utilization of spare parts, but the data concerning these wagons is very vague and uncertain. It can be estimated that in 1925, there were about twenty such wagons. The number decreased over time, so in 1931, after the completion of the final reorganisation, only seven surpluss wagons were accounted for.

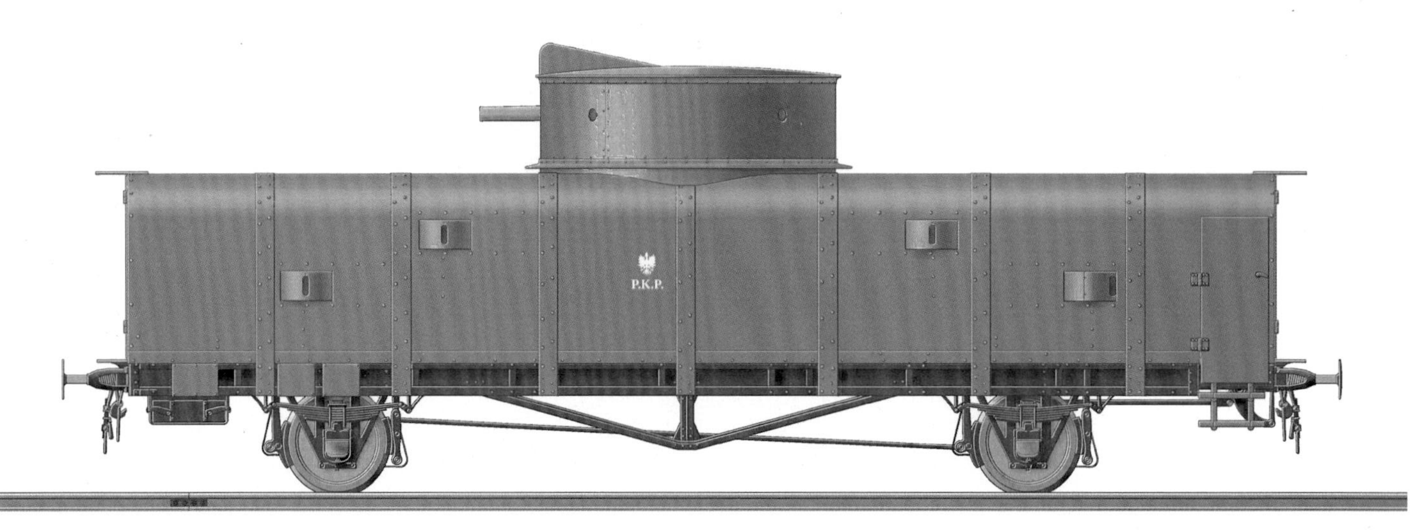

Artillery wagon 402633 (armoured in 1919, it served with "Paderewski", "Groźny" *and* "Hallerczyk"*). It was later converted into an assault wagon.*

A cropped image of the "Hallerczyk", *taken in summer 1920 – artillery wagon number 402633 is enlarged.*

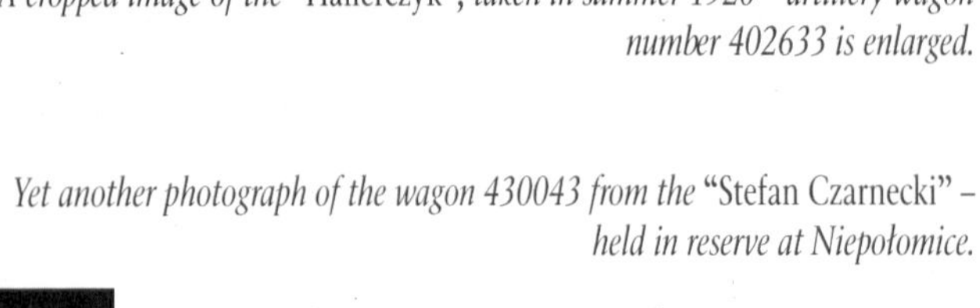

Yet another photograph of the wagon 430043 from the "Stefan Czarnecki" *– held in reserve at Niepołomice.*